The Patchwork Planner

Flower Power

Size 125 × 125cm (49 × 49in.) 1991. Design shown on page 12, figure 15.

The Patchwork Planner

350 Original Designs For Traditional Patchwork

Birte Hilberg

David & Charles

JAW GF EA OX

The Patchwork Planner
350 Original Designs for Traditional Patchwork
Birte Hilberg

Photography by Paul Biddle

A DAVID & CHARLES BOOK
Copyright Text and Designs © Birte Hilberg 1993
Photographs © David & Charles 1993
First published 1993

A catalogue record for this book is available from the British
Library.

ISBN 0 7153 0008 3

Typeset by ICON, Exeter
and printed in Hong Kong by Imago Publishing Ltd
for David & Charles
Brunel House Newton Abbot Devon

27.95

Contents

To Claus

Arctic Sunset

Tablecloth. Size 130 x 130 cm (51 x 51 in.) 1991

Introduction

This book is intended as a new source of inspiration for quilt makers and other crafts people who employ geometric patterns in their work. It shows some 350 new designs, drawn from a much bigger collection, developed during my study of how simple, square patterns – throughout this book referred to as "tiles" – create complex designs when joined together according to a few very simple rules, either on their own or mixed with other tiles.

In selecting the designs, attempts have been made to cover as wide a spectrum as possible, ranging from the delicate to the bold and encompassing motifs suitable for all kinds of projects, whether the requirement is for full-size quilts, wall hangings, baby quilts or any other patchwork item. Many designs are shown in large units, which immediately reveals secondary patterns and gives a better impression of the finished work.

The designs are all new in the sense that to my knowledge, they have not previously appeared in books or magazines. They are however at the same time traditional in their style, and they *could* have been created a long time ago. Some of the tiles may resemble those used in well-known designs like Drunkard's Path and World Without End, but they have then tended to be associated with these designs only. This book will show that traditional-style tiles have a lot more to offer.

When studying the designs on the following pages, it may sometimes be helpful to turn the book by 90 degrees. It is amazing how a design can change completely when seen horizontally rather than vertically. Also, it may be easier to see how tiles interact to create large scale designs if you look at some of the designs from farther away.

I am a hand-piecing fanatic, but a machine-piecing devotee should not be put off. A combination of the two techniques may actually be optimal – hand-piece the tiles, and use the machine to join them. Instructions on the cutting of templates and on piecing have however been excluded, as other books cover these topics very well. I have found *The Quiltmaker's Handbook* and *The Second Quiltmaker's Handbook* by Michael James (Prentice-Hall, 1978 and 1981) and *Quiltmaking in Patchwork & Appliqué* by Michele Walker (Ebury Press, 1985) particularly useful.

The finished works shown are designed and hand-pieced by Birte Hilberg unless otherwise stated. All works are quilted by hand.

Designing Blocks on a Home Computer

The four-patch, five-patch and nine-patch technique has been used in patchwork for several generations. It is useful because it makes piecing patterns of a geometrical nature simpler by reducing the job to smaller, more manageable blocks. Several books on basic patchwork techniques describe the process in detail and include examples of traditional designs made this way (see *The Quilter's Album of Blocks and Borders* by Jinny Beyer, EPM Publications Inc., 1980).

The study that eventually led to the writing of this book started in 1984 with the following question, intended more as a joke than as a serious query: "How many different 4 by 4 blocks can be made if we choose to work with just one basic tile, namely one containing one black and one white triangle?" Numerous books will show examples of such designs, but the number of different designs is limited, and the idea behind the question was that there ought to be many more. Answering the question turned out to be far from trivial and my husband was "employed" to write a computer program to speed up the analysis.

This initial project uncovered two surprises: One was that even if care was taken to eliminate blocks that were simple mirror images or translations of other blocks, the answer turned out to be "Hundreds". The other surprise was that many of the designs never shown in textbooks were actually very attractive and well suited for patchwork. Being able to see a large number of blocks together gave me an immediate impression of secondary patterns. But a single event turned the project into a passion: it was when I realised that if the triangles contained so much undiscovered potential, it ought to be worth spending a few more hours experimenting with other basic tiles.

This book then contains some of the results of seven years of development of this idea. All work has been done using a small computer system; without it, the whole project would have been unrealistic. The program runs on an IBM PC (any 80286 based VGA machine or better will do), and it is still being modified more than once a month to encompass new ideas. A library of some 500 basic tiles has been created; some of them are well known to patchworkers, but most have been "invented" for the purpose of this project. The program will work with any number of different tiles in one design, but even with very few tiles at a time, the variety of designs achievable is almost limitless. Except for the kaleidoscope designs described later, most of the designs shown in this book contain just one or two different tiles.

On top of the computer's obvious advantage in speed, patience and ability to store large volumes of data, it has one more facility that has played an important role during the study; it can in no time at all show a design in any number of colour combinations, using plain colours or various lines and dots to symbolise printed fabrics. In order to judge the potential of a design fairly, it is essential to see it in more than just a few colour combinations. The three designs on the opposite page are intended to illustrate this: The basic square has been built from four T-shaped figures. Neither the black and white version in figure 1 nor the blue-green-yellow version of the design in figure 2 would appear to contain anything interesting, while the red-blue versions in figure 3 of exactly the same design shows a wreath that could be exploited to good effect. The moral of the story is that it is all too easy to discard good ideas simply because the colours are wrong, but at least the use of the computer makes this **less** likely.

When selecting designs for this book, it has been necessary to concentrate on those that can be sensibly shown in black, white and shades of grey. Some 55 designs are shown in colours as they appear on the computer screen. A few are even shown in two different colour combinations, thus illustrating how the choice of colour can highlight different aspects of the design. But whether the illustrations are in colour or not, it is important to remember that the pictures are intended to highlight the potential of a design. More often than not, the designs will benefit if more colours are added. Furthermore, when judging the colour designs, please bear in mind that the seam lines and the grid shown may tend to influence the perception of the picture.

Fig. 1

Fig. 2

Fig. 3

The Tiles

The 77 different tiles used to create the designs found in this book are all shown on pages 189–191. The majority of tiles are so simple that drawing the templates will cause no problem at all. But to ease the way, tiles have been split into 4 groups:

Tiles number 100–199 are the most basic. They are all drawn in a simple square, as shown in figure 4.

Fig. 4

Tiles number 200–299 have in common that to draw them you need to find the midpoint of the sides of the square. They are most easily drawn if you use a grid of 4 squares, as shown in figure 5.

Fig. 5

Tiles number 300–399 are all based upon squares where the sides are divided into 3. To draw them, start with a 9-square grid, as shown in figure 6.

Fig. 6

Tiles number 400–499 are then based upon squares with the sides divided into 4, i.e. start with a 16-square grid, as shown in figure 7.

Fig. 7

The only times when a pocket calculator may be required are when you draw tiles 270, 275, 276 or 277. The centre for the required segment of the circle is located outside the square. As shown, it lies on the extension of one of the sides, and the distance to the nearest corner of the square is three-quarters of the length of the side.

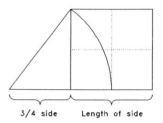

There are a few tiles where it may not be obvious where a line starts or ends. Typical examples are tiles 291, 389 and 454. The trick here is to extend the line all the way to the edge of the square. The extension will always cross the edge in an "obvious" place: in tile 389 it hits the midpoint of the side.

Each chapter in the book concentrates on a small family of tiles, which is shown at the bottom of the first page of the chapter. The full list of tiles required to make a design is indicated in the margin next to the design.

It should be noted that when it comes to piecing, it may help a lot to add a few more lines within some of the tiles. Suggested additional lines are shown as dotted lines in the tile index. The underlying principle is that the more open an angle is, the easier is the piecing, but exactly when and where to divide depends on individual skills and piecing method.

From Tile to Design

In principle, one could build designs from the library of basic tiles simply by picking a number of tiles, and then start putting them together and changing them around until something attractive appears. A number of the designs have actually been made that way, but a more systematic approach is clearly more effective. In the end, the most productive method of studying a tile (or a small set of tiles) has been to build into the computer programme a fixed set of a dozen or so different ways of assembling tiles. Each of these techniques involves joining a few tiles randomly into a rectangle, and then use this rectangle for building the design. Taking each technique one at a time, I go through a large number of designs on the screen. Experience has shown that it is impossible to say which of the various techniques is best: any mix of tiles tends to have its own characteristics that can only be discovered through experimentation. Even then, the majority of designs will turn out to be of no value. A few will be excellent, ready for use, but more often they will contain interesting features. Most of the designs in this book are the result of taking inspiration from such features and developing them further.

To illustrate some of the principles employed, let us study the tile used for Flower Power, the design on page 2. The tile is shown below in figure 8. It is made from 3 strips of equal width plus the two small triangular corners.

To create a 4-patch, the computer joined 4 of these in a **2 by 2** square (figure 9) – **a basic set** of tiles.

Figure 10 shows the same basic set of tiles, but with shadings added. Note that the upper left and the lower right tiles have been coloured using 2 shadings only, while the other 2 tiles have been coloured differently, using 4 shadings.

To make a block from this basic set of tiles, the most common techniques are simply to repeat it, mirror it or rotate it. Almost three-quarters of the designs shown in this book are made in one of these ways. Figure 11 shows a design created by repeating figure 10. To make a mirror pattern, imagine for example 2 mirrors placed vertically along the borders of figure 10, meeting in the lower right-hand corner. What could then be seen in the mirrors is the mirrored block shown in figure 12. As an example of a rotated block, imagine rotating figure 10 first 90, then 180 and finally 270 degrees around its top right-hand corner: the four drawings put together produce the rotated pattern shown in figure 13.

Fig. 8

Fig. 9

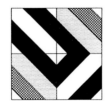

Fig. 10

Another way of making a block is to choose 8 different orientations for the basic tile or tiles, placing them in a 2 by 4 rectangle as shown in figure 14, and mirroring that rectangle once to produce the basic block shown in figure 15. Taking the idea even further, the computer can at times create striking blocks by placing all 16 tiles in the block at random, as shown in figure 16.

When 4 identical blocks are put together in an 8 by 8 square, a **secondary pattern** is formed where the blocks meet. This is illustrated opposite, where the blocks in figures 12, 13, 15 and 16 have been used again; it can be something new, like the big X in

figure 17. It can, as in figures 18 and 19, be a repetition of the basic block (in which case the result is always pleasing to look at); or it can have interesting new dimensions, as in figure 20. There are even times when the secondary pattern is more interesting than the block itself, and one could consider using it as the basic block. Figure 21 is the same as figure 17, but shifted to make better use of the secondary pattern.

Just as there are several ways of making a block from a basic set of tiles, there are several ways of putting blocks together. As an example, figure 22 shows 4 identical mirrored blocks which have been assembled by rotating them.

Fig. 11

Fig. 12

Fig. 13

Fig. 14

Fig. 15

Fig. 16

Fig. 17

Fig. 18

Fig. 19

Fig. 20

Fig. 21

Fig. 22

Fig. 23

Fig. 24

We can use the Flower Power design in figure 15 to illustrate a couple more ways of creating a design from a block. One is to make the lower half of the design a mirror image of the top half, as in figure 23.

The other is slightly more elaborate: Draw two diagonal lines across an 8 by 8 square, as in figure 24 (the same as figure 19). Pick one of the four triangles, and use 4 copies of that to create a square. Figure 25 shows what happens if the top triangle in figure 24 is chosen. Had we drawn the diagonal lines in figure 24 across the middle 8 by 8 block rather than through the left-hand block, the square design shown in figure 26 would have emerged.

Fig. 25   *Fig. 26*

The outcome of this method, referred to earlier as the kaleidoscope design, is very unpredictable, especially when using rotating blocks, but the result can be quite fascinating and is well suited for all "square" projects such as play mats for toddlers, a centre for a medallion quilt or even enlarged to fit a double bed. It could also be treated like one big block and be repeated like the one shown in figure 27.

Fig. 27

Finally, figure 29 shows what happens if a basic set of tiles like the one in figure 28 is first mirrored once to the right and then repeated many times, and figure 30 shows the effect of first mirroring the 2 tiles in figure 28 downward, and then repeating that one many times. And last of all, figure 31 shows an example of putting 96 tiles together completely at random.

Fig. 28　　　　*Fig. 29*　　　　*Fig. 30*

Fig. 31

1

S p o t   O n :
T r i a n g l e s

This chapter is devoted entirely to simple variations of triangles. As mentioned earlier, a trivial question about the number of possible patterns derived only from black and white triangles set the ball rolling, but only one example of these designs has been included – the Flying Geese variations shown in page 18. This was the inspiration for the multicoloured panels found on page 19.

Three further variations of the triangle motif are illustrated. Pages 20 through 23 demonstrate the effect of dividing one of the triangles into two (tile 113), thus producing a three-colour tile. The mirrored blocks on page 21 create large Windmill type designs when they are rotated. Using a tile where one

of the two small triangles is subdivided once more (tile 227) has led to the Spot On wall hanging (page 25). The designs are bold, and they call for the use of bright colours.

The second variation can be found on the following 6 pages, where I have put a small triangle on top of one or both of the big triangles (as in tile 301). The technique sounds simple enough, but the effect is much more intricate, and the designs lighter and more elegant.

Finally, pages 32 and 33 show a variation of the traditional Attic Window tile (tile 463). This tile has quite a lot of potential, and it pops up several times throughout the book.

Tile 113

Tile 227

Tile 301

Tile 463

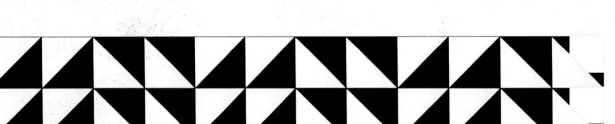

220

102

Flying Geese Variation

A set of 16 separate panels fills one wall in our hall. Together they form a
colour wash, from black and red at the bottom of the stairs to white and
yellow at the top. The design has been repeated in half size to
enhance the overall effect.

Individual panels are between 24 cm (9.4 in.) and 47 cm (18.5 in.) wide

Finished 1988

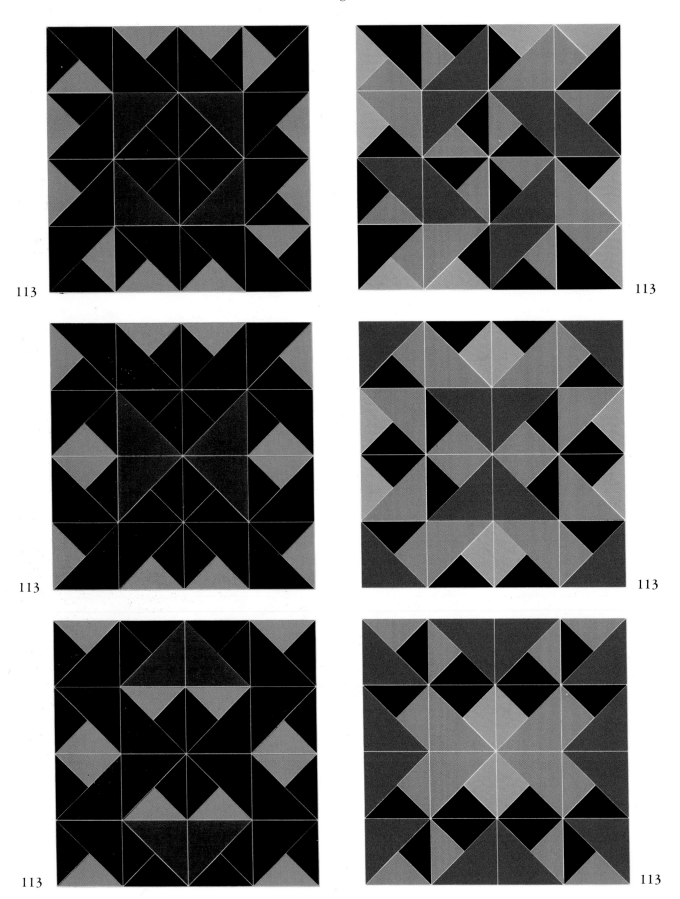

113

113

113

113

113

113

113

113

Flower Garden

This quilt was a commission from my son, age 11, who selected the
design and specified that it should be made in primary colours. The quilting design by Mrs Audrey Griffin consists of lilies, barley and poppies cor-
responding to the blue, yellow and red colours.
Size 176 × 144 cm (69 × 56 in.) 1989

113

This design is based on one mirrored 4 by 4 block, repeated six times in a
rotating manner (like figure 22). To show the big overlapping squares better,
the design has been extended by one tile in all four directions.

227

227

227

Spot On

Note that this wall hanging, using the centre design on page 24, could
equally well be mounted "horizontally", i.e. turned 90 degrees. The effect
would then be like arrows, showing the way out!
Size 106 × 106 cm (41 × 41 in.) 1990

220

220

220

220

220

220

301

301

303

303

303

303

301

301

301

301

301

301

463

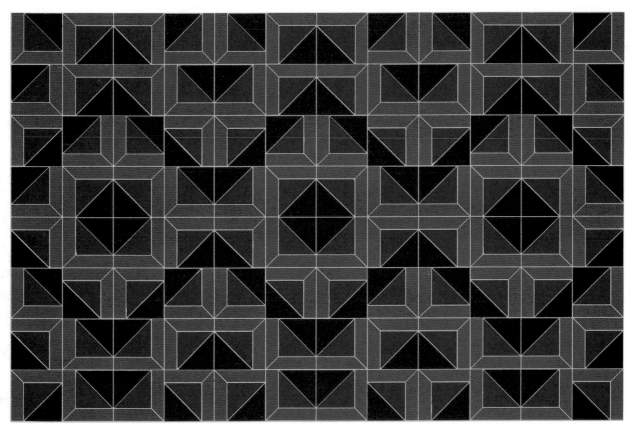

463

463

463

Peace by Piece

All colours of the EC flags are represented
Schola Europaea, Luxembourg
Size 170 × 150 cm (67 × 59 in.) 1990
Photo by Raymond Faber, Luxembourg

2

Playtime:
Twisted Ribbons

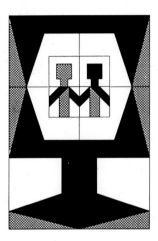

T his chapter is dedicated to two of the "twisted ribbon" type tiles. While number 341 on its own can be seen as two ribbons wrapped around each other, number 362 supports this effect, and creates an effect similar to that of tile 341 when four of them are together forming a frame (see page 45). The empty spaces are well suited for large pictures, be it a bouquet of flowers cut from a printed fabric, a teddy bear cut from prints intended for baby quilts, a child's first crayon drawing on fabric, or perhaps an elegant silk painting.

It is interesting to note that number 341 should normally not be used on its own – the outcome is usually much too "busy". But as this chapter shows, when it is mixed with simple stripes, a large number of fascinating designs can be made.

Many of the following designs are based upon the kaleidoscope design, which was described on pages 14 and 15. One use of these designs could be as intricate centres in medallions quilts, or you might want to use them for baby quilts. In the making of the "Playtime" baby quilt (page 42), rather a lot of "rabbit" fabric had to be purchased – 4 metres (4½ yards) to be precise – but the designs on page 37 will

not require quite as much. Alternatively, if the designs are enlarged for bed quilts, there will be large open areas, pleading to be quilted!

Towards the end of the chapter, tile 364 becomes prominent. It can for instance be seen as a leaf, creating an effect like hawthorn or holly. (Note that tile 364 has been made by mirroring tile 341 through the diagonal; it is not that obvious!)

The border designs on the last page introduce the first curved tile, one that will be studied in detail in the next chapter. A few more borders can be found in later chapters, but many more can be created simply by focusing on one or two rows across or columns down a design. If you need to turn a corner with such a border design, you will have to mitre the corners, precisely as happens in the kaleidoscope designs.

Tile 341

Tile 362

Tile 364

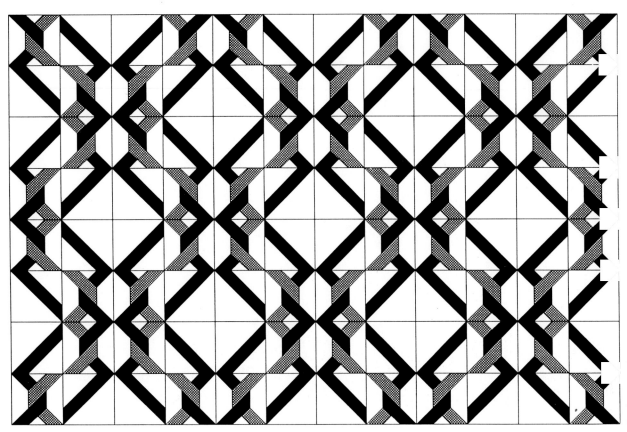

320
341

321
341

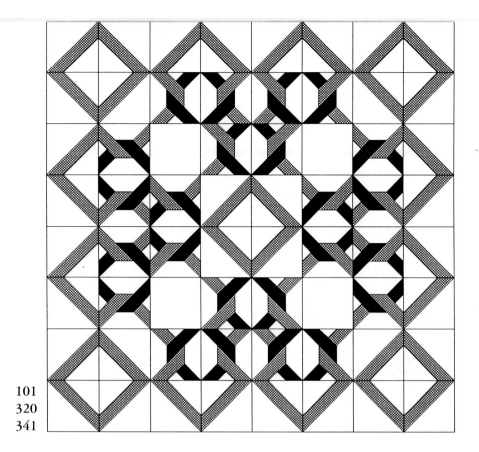

101
320
341

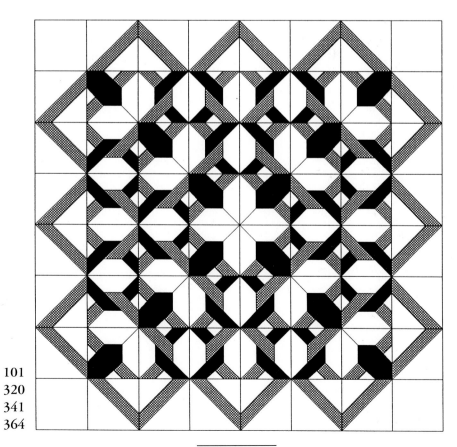

101
320
341
364

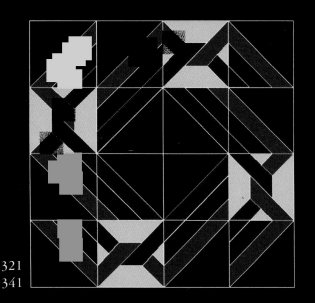

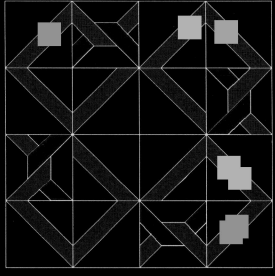

321
341

320
341

321
322
341
365

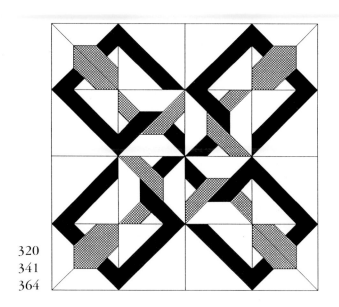

320
341
364

320
321
341

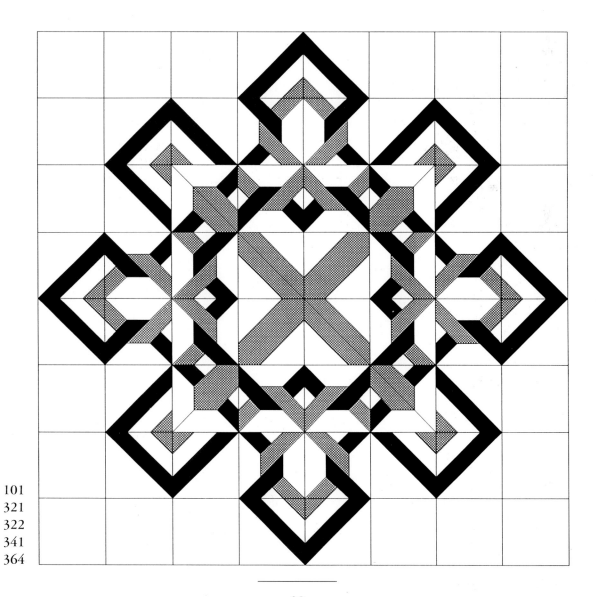

101
321
322
341
364

101
320
341
364

Design for the *Playtime* baby quilt

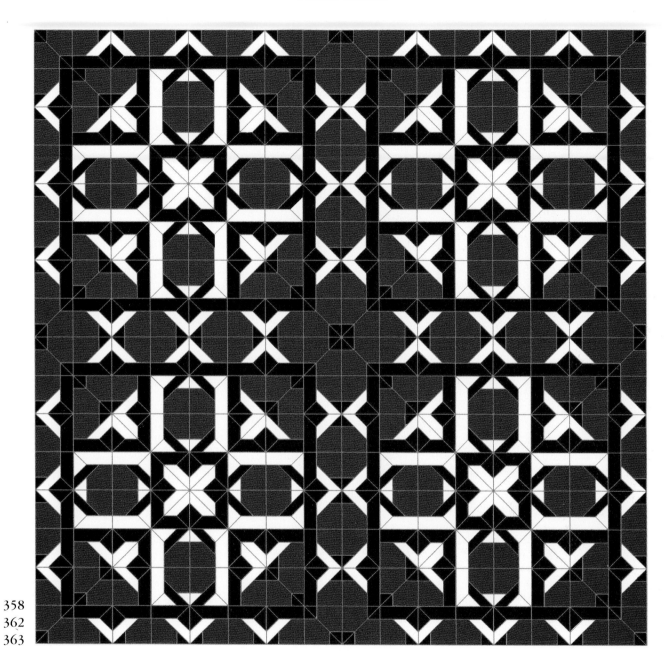

358
362
363

Design for the *Daydreams* baby quilt

Daydreams was made from just one-quarter of this design

Playtime

Size 125 × 125 cm (49 × 49 in.) 1990
Design on page 40. Similar designs can be found on page 37

Daydreams

Baby quilt. Size 118 × 118 cm (46 × 46 in.) 1990
Design on page 41

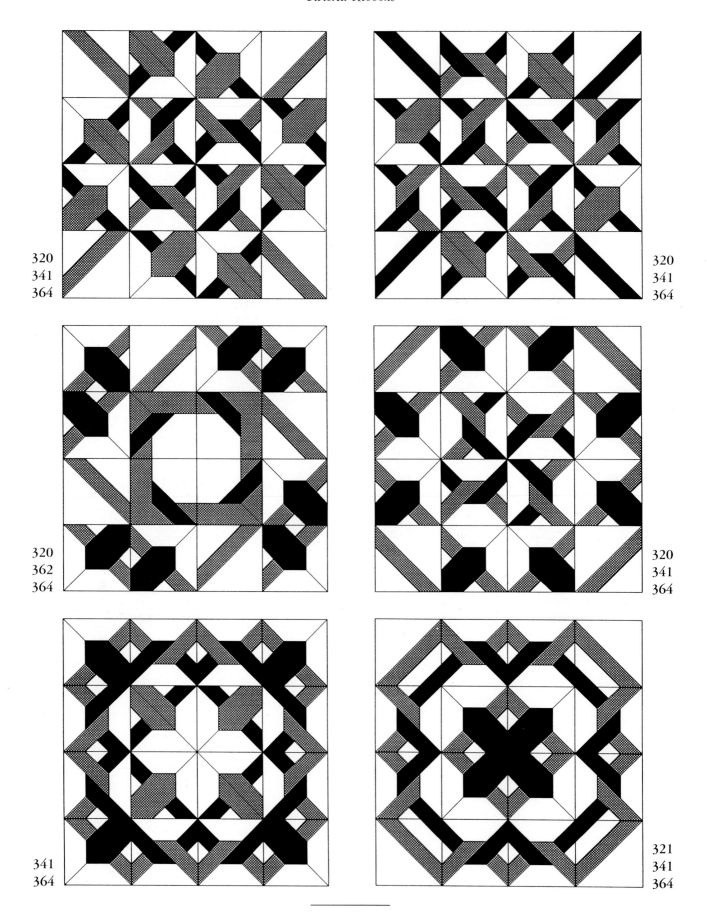

320
341
364

320
341
364

320
362
364

320
341
364

341
364

321
341
364

362
364

362
364

320
362
364

320
362
364

362
364

362
364

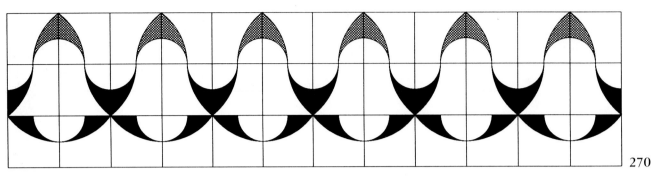

270

270
341

270
341

270
341

3

Pink Romance: Curves and Ribbons

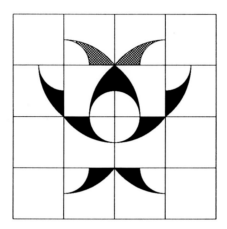

T his chapter should fulfil the dreams of every sentimental soul who wishes to make something really beautiful, romantic and elegant.

Let us first look at tile number 335. It can be seen as a two-colour ribbon, twisted once, and is taken from the same family as the tiles studied in the previous chapter. Its use is however very different, giving an impression of garlands of attractive flowers and leaves, lighter and more delicate than the twisted band designs shown earlier. Another difference is that you must be more careful with your choice of colours and with the quilting because the shape of the "background" is unattractive. My solution has been to choose colours to emphasise the "garlands" rather than the background, and to use a criss-cross quilting pattern so that the distance between the quilt lines matches the width of the "ribbon". The effect can be seen in the finished pieces on page 51: the white areas fade away, and the desired effect has been achieved. This is the first time we are confronted with this phenomena, but it is fairly common, and you should keep it in mind throughout the book.

The second tile to be studied is number 270, a close partner to number 335 among the curved designs. Introduced on page 48 to help create border designs, it is one of my favourite tiles. It may be a bit tricky to piece, but it has proven exceptionally versatile, whether used alone or in the company of other tiles. It is also the most successful tile, creating a larger number of attractive designs than any other tile. This chapter shows only a small selection of the types of design that can be obtained, and you are encouraged to study it further. Note however that it is slightly more complicated to draw than most other tiles used in this book. Turn to page 10 for help.

Page 55 shows how a detail from within a large quilt can be used as border to create a soft finishing touch. This idea may prove particularly useful for the designs found in this chapter. The last three pages of the chapter show my favourite tile in combinations with squares and triangles. The effect it creates gives strong and exciting designs of surprising complexity.

Tile 270

Tile 335

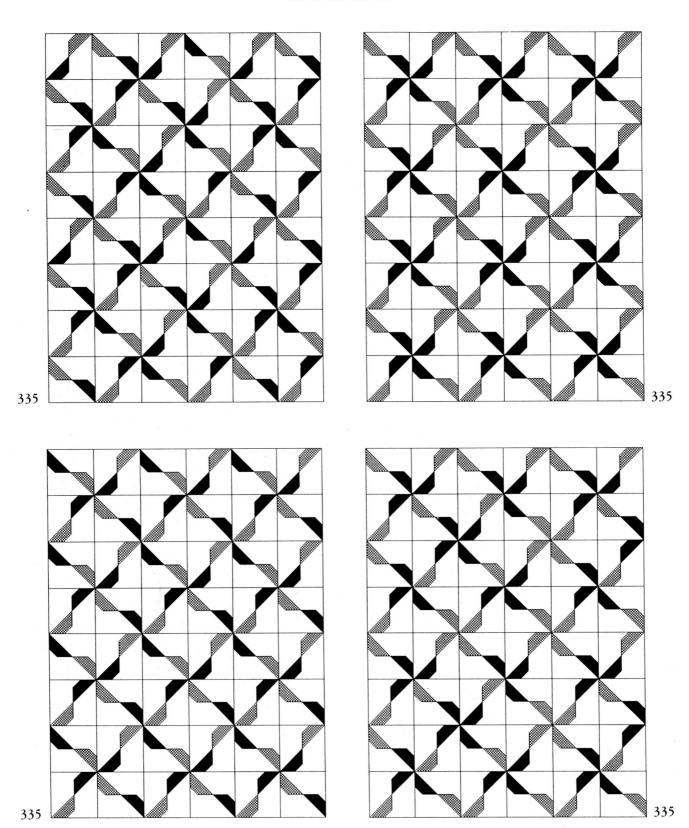

335

335

335

335

Pink Romance

Single quilt. Size 200 × 156 cm (78 × 61 in.) 1990
Design on page 50
Two cushions. Size 50 × 50 cm (20 × 20 in.)
Designs on page 80

270

270

270

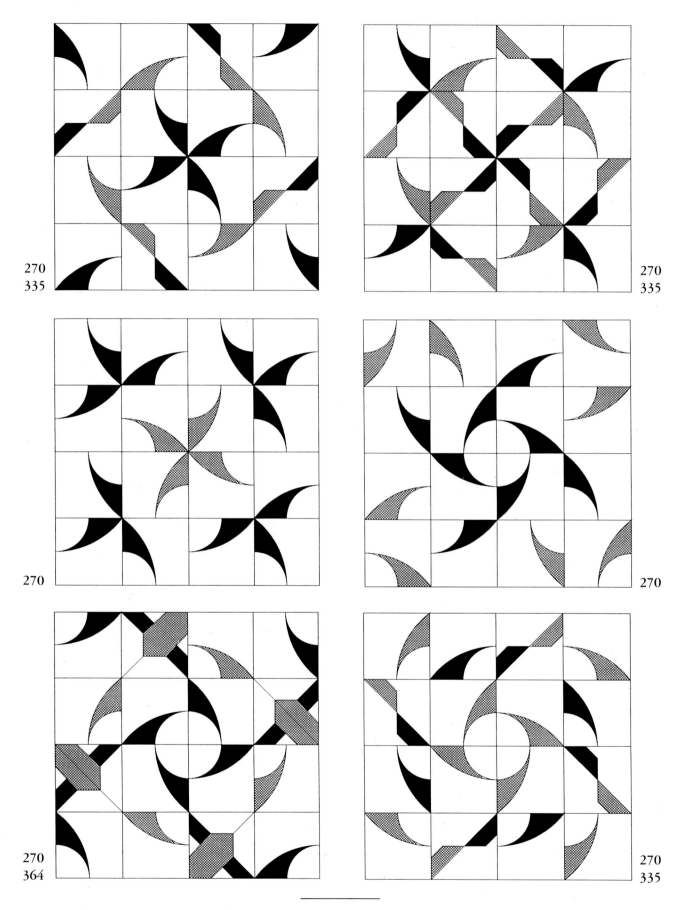

270
335

270
335

270

270

270
364

270
335

101
270
364

270
335

270
335

270
335

270
335

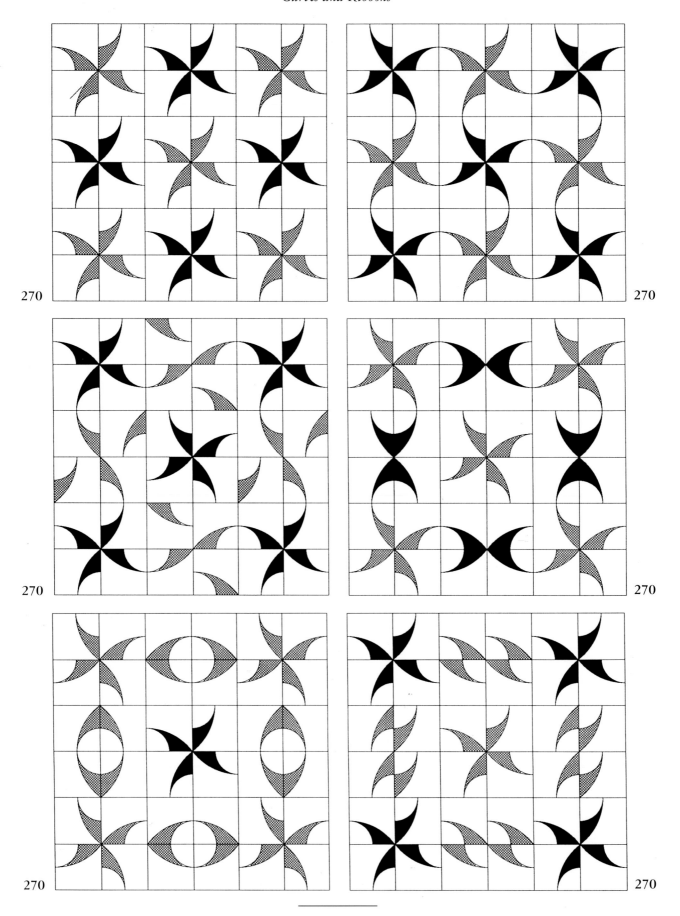

270

270

270

270

270

270

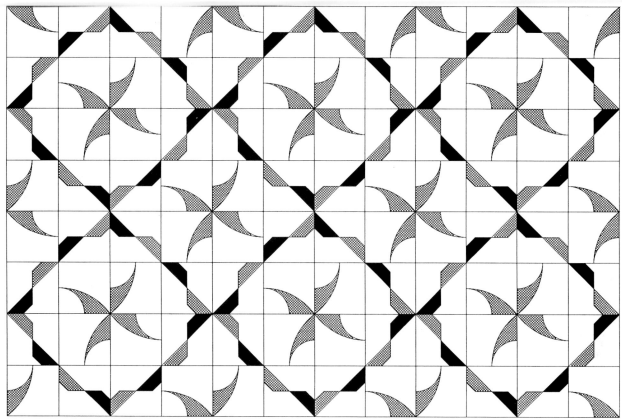

270
335

270
335

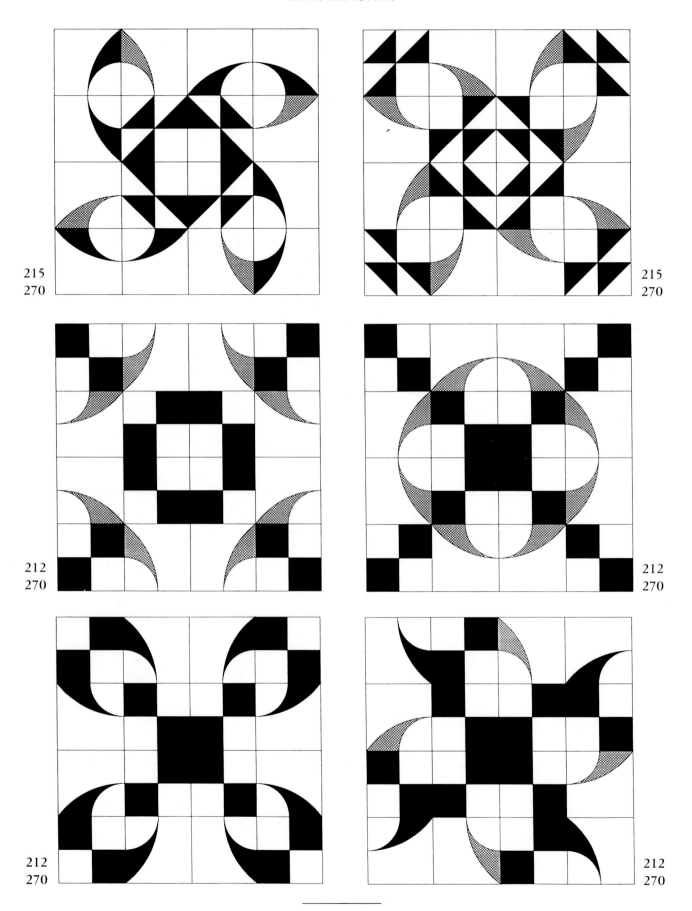

215
270

215
270

212
270

212
270

212
270

212
270

215
270

215
270

4

Split Personalities: Curves

So far, we have encountered only one tile with curved seams. In this and the following chapter, six new "curved" tiles will be introduced.

The basic tile is number 275. It is a simplified version of number 270, which was used extensively in chapter 3. It is of little interest when used on its own (the three designs in this chapter plus the borders on page 78 just about exhaust my list), but it comes to life when mixed with triangles and squares. Where tile 270 tends to create elegant designs, the simplified version leads to bolder and stronger designs, calling for contrasting colours. The blocks shown on pages 70 and 71 are typical examples.

They are particularly well suited as single blocks in cushions, but whereas the mirrored blocks on page 70 can also be repeated for larger items, the rotating blocks on page 71 tend to lose their appeal when more identical blocks appear together.

While I was studying some simple variations of tile 275, one day little faces suddenly appeared on the computer screen. When I further discovered (purely by chance) that tile 265 could be used for hair, bows or even bodies, making people became quite a passion. But I have found it is important to limit myself; if there are too many people in one wall hanging, it becomes less interesting and gives only a blurred impression.

Tile 226

Tile 270

Tile 275

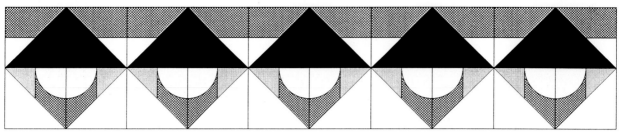

226
280

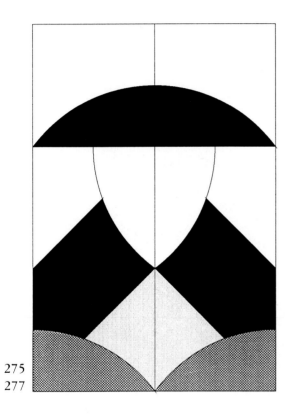

275
277

265
277

Designs for *Ordinary People* and *Split Personalities*

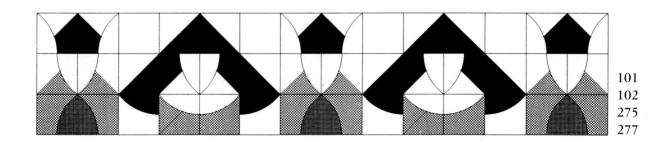

101
102
275
277

269
432
434

269
432
434

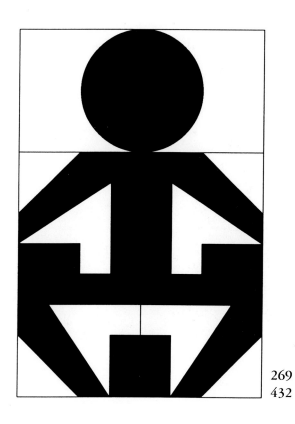

269
432

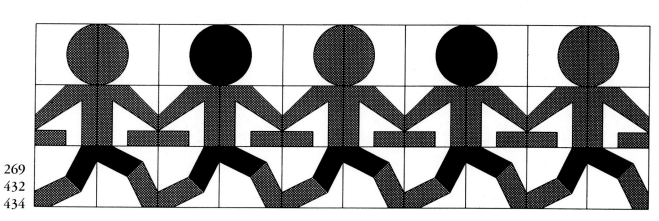

269
432
434

Ordinary People

This wall hanging includes friends, public figures, sporting heroes, the man
who got very seasick on the boat to Denmark, etc.
Size 120 × 101 cm (47 × 39 in.) 1990

Split Personalities

Wall hanging
Size 90 × 62 cm (36 × 24 in.) 1990

275

275

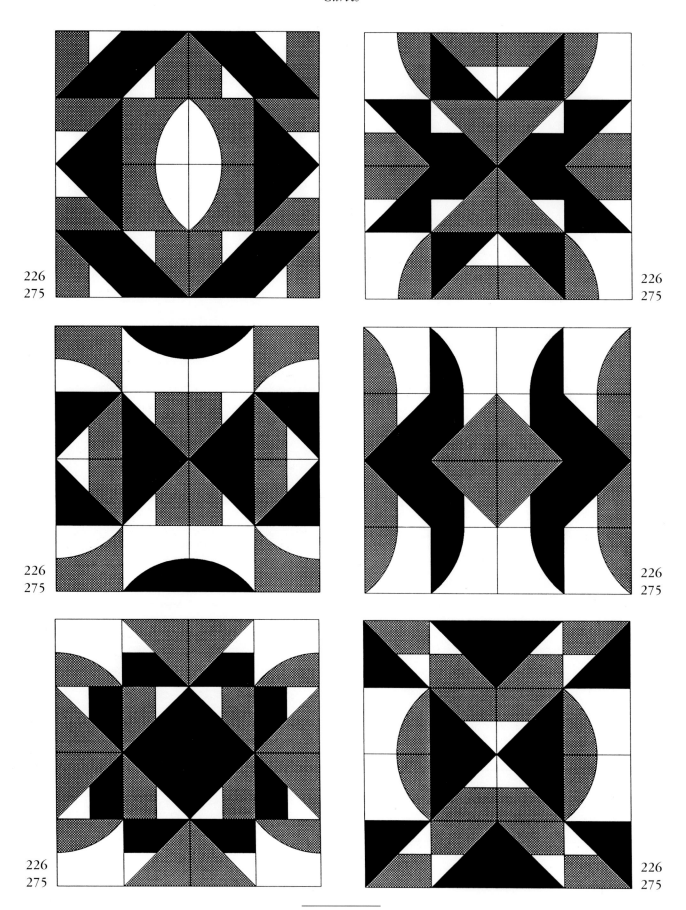

226
275

226
275

226
275

226
275

226
275

226
275

226
275

226
275

226
275

226
275

226
275

226
275

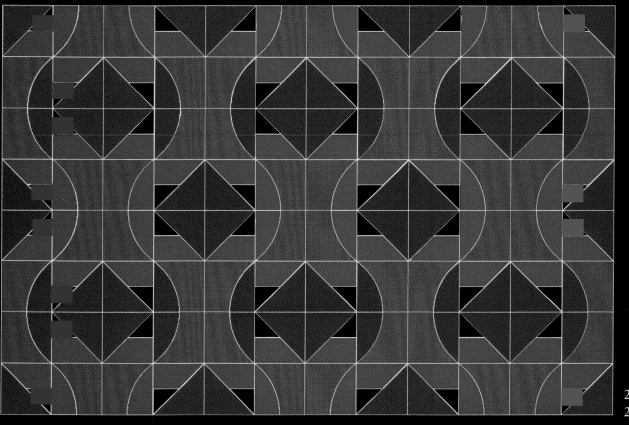

211
212
275

211
275

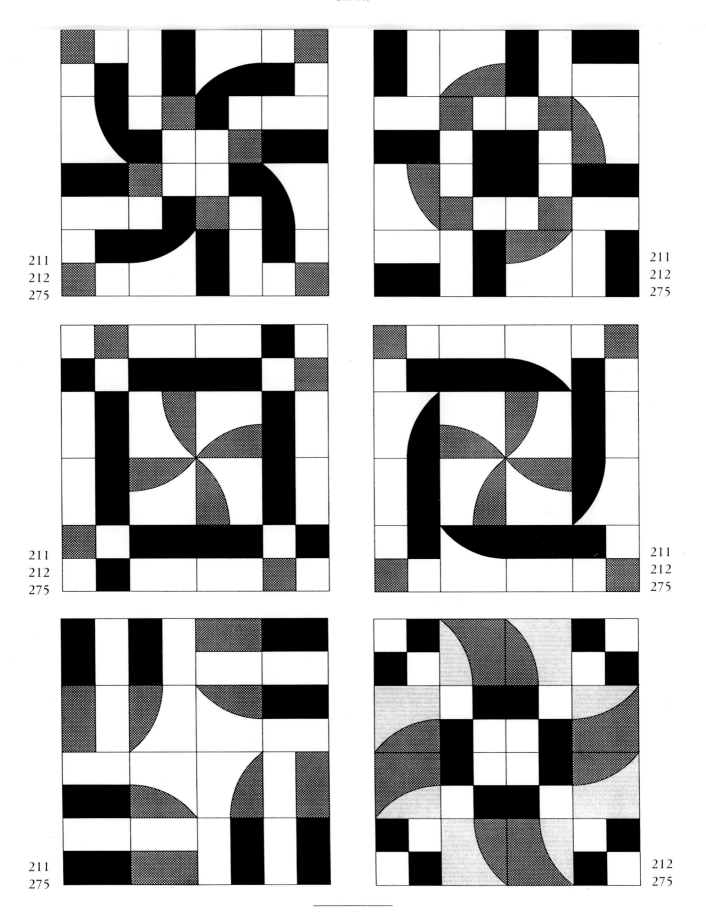

211
212
275

211
212
275

211
212
275

211
212
275

211
275

212
275

275

This design has been extended by 1 tile in all 4 directions

211
212
275

211
275

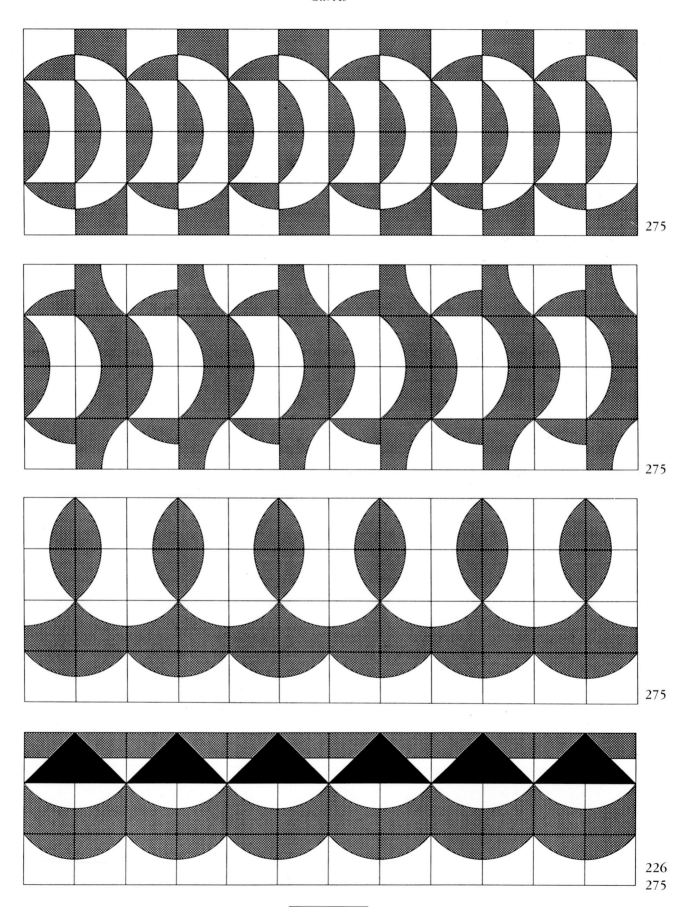

275

275

275

226
275

5

Blackbirds:
Curves and Points

Virtually every design in this chapter has tile number 273 as the key element. It is an elongated version of the tile 270 that was the feature of chapter 3, and it shares many of the properties of that tile. It produces almost as many good designs, but where 270 was useful alone, 273 needs support. Two of the supporting tiles which suit 273 are 278, which differs from the Drunkard's Path tile in the radius of its quarter circle, and the pointed tile 235 that is used to produce designs resembling flowers and bells. Other great supporters are 275, 276 and 212 – the latter is used frequently throughout the book; it is such a "simple" tile and blends in

so well that you may sometimes have to look twice to see that it's there!

The only design that does not include 273 is the birds designs on pages 83–85, which uses the tile traditionally known from the Drunkard's Path design. Drunkard's Path is one of the best-known "curved" designs, often the only example given. It has been a surprise to find that after many hours of search, Blackbirds was the only other design of particular interest using this tile. The versions of Blackbirds shown on pages 85 and 88 (the two blocks at the top) are more elegant and the white background area on the latter two designs can be used for extensive quilting.

Tile 212

Tile 235

Tile 270

Tile 273

Tile 275

Tile 276

Tile 278

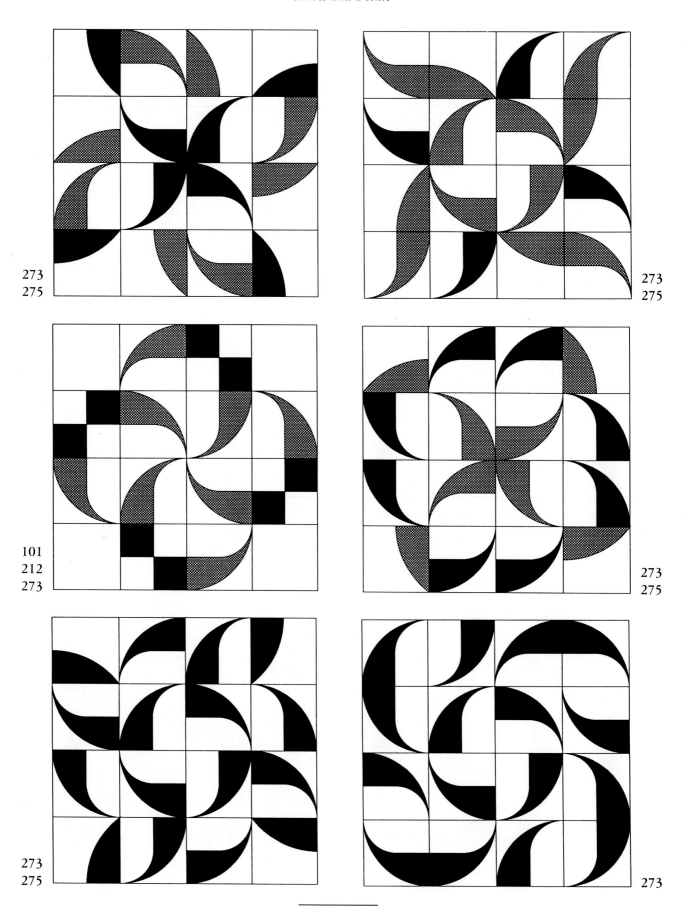

273
275

273
275

101
212
273

273
275

273
275

273

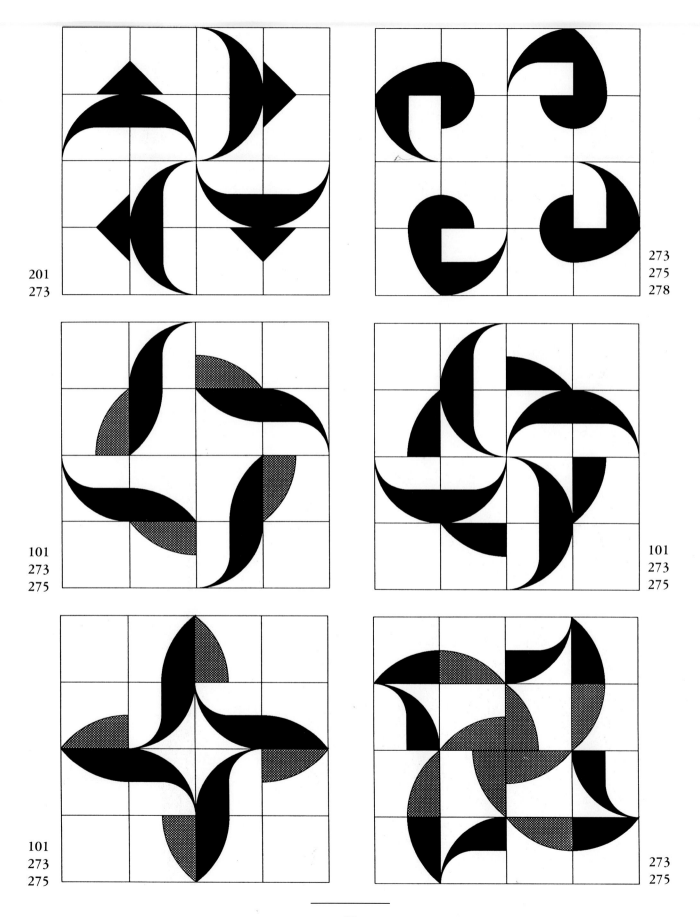

201
273

273
275
278

101
273
275

101
273
275

101
273
275

273
275

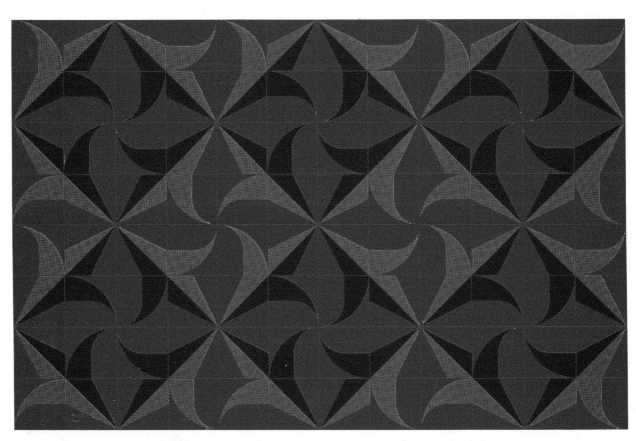

235
273

235
273

Marianne's Swallows

Bedspread by Marianne Bondo Hoff, 1992
Size 220 × 200 cm (87 × 78 in.)
Design on page 85

Blackbirds

Wall hanging. Size 108 × 84 cm (42 × 33 in.) 1987
Privately owned
Design on page 85

273
278

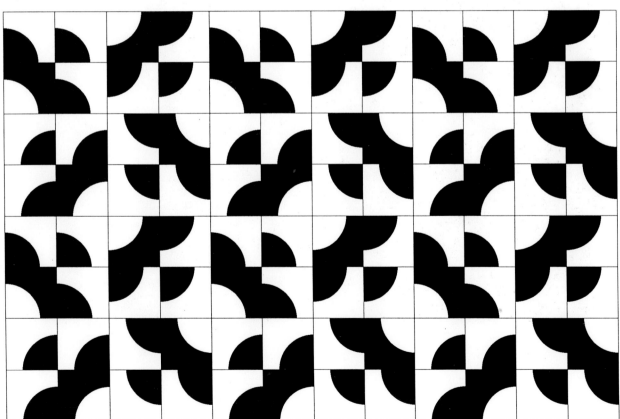

310

235
273
278

235
273
278

Wedding Bells design

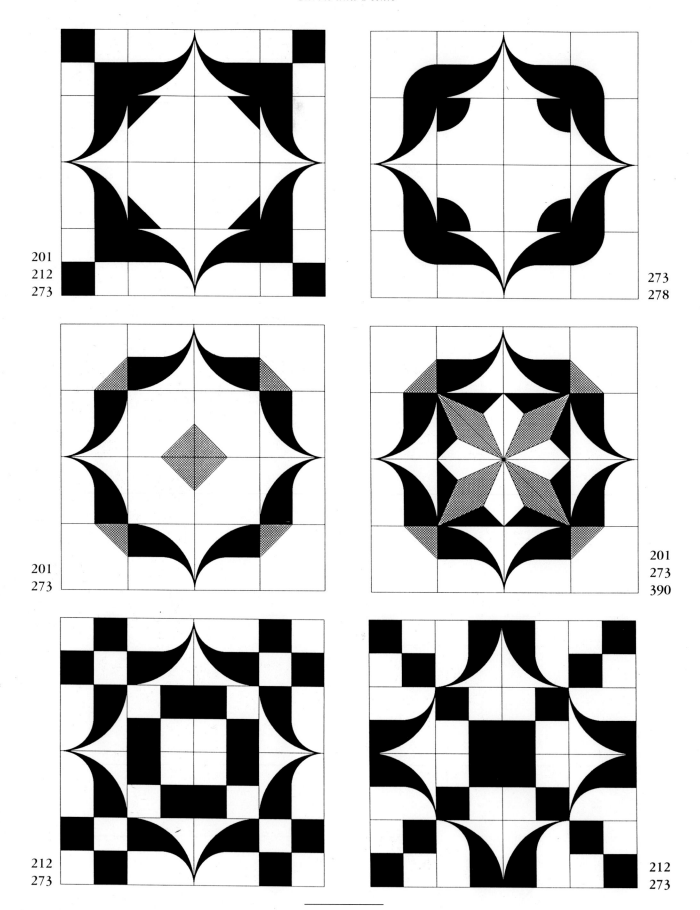

201
212
273

273
278

201
273

201
273
390

212
273

212
273

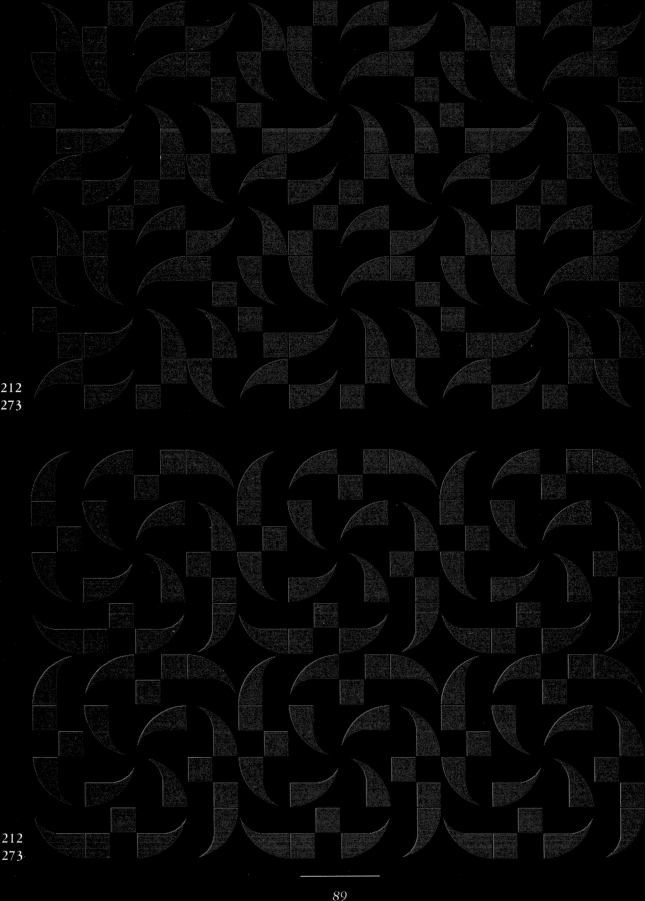

212
273

212
273

273
275

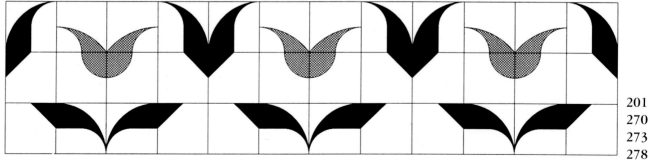

201
270
273
278

270
276

270
273
276

273
276

273
276

273
276

273
276

6

Way In:
Stripes and Triangles

et us leave curved designs behind and instead look at triangles once more to see how a few stripes can help to create designs of a completely different nature to the original ones. Where designs so far may have called for the use of strong colours, this chapter shows designs that call for plenty of different colours. I have always found designs that gave an impresssion of several layers of designs on top of each other particularly fascinating, and many designs in this chapter have a potential for this effect, as long as the colours are chosen with that in mind.

Not all of the finished works shown on the following pages have been worked out at the computer. Instead, what tended to happen was that a detail in a design caught my eye and I ended up building a design around that detail. A typical example was

when an arrow appeared while I was working with tiles 113 and 321 – as in the designs on page 96. The arrow idea turned into Way In, a wall hanging that gave hours of fun trying to fit in as many arrows as possible and at the same time focusing on the weaving of the arrows.

The arrows theme can be found in most of the designs in this chapter. In some, it has been made to stand out, while in others it has been toned down. It all depends on the use of colours.

The designs on pages 104, 105 and 107 are all made using the 2 by 4 method mentioned on pages 12 and 14. To the extent that we can ever generalize about how designs should be used, I would suggest that these designs are best used in wall hangings. But – once again – they call for the use of plenty of colours.

Tile 113

Tile 321

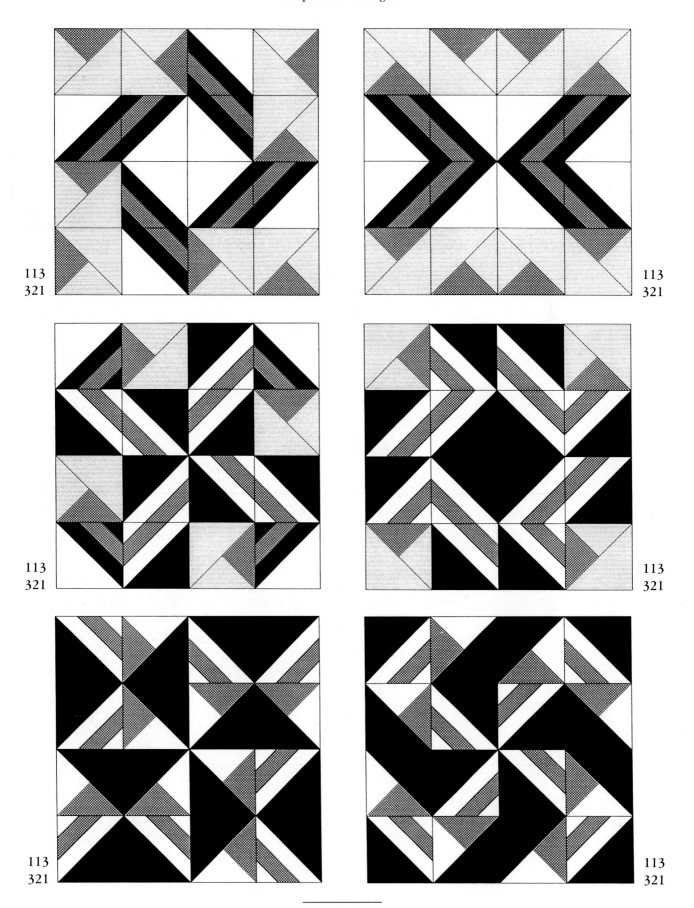

113
321

113
321

113
321

113
321

113
321

113
321

Way In

Wall hanging. Size 115 × 98 cm (45 × 38 in.) 1988
Machine pieced

321
324

321
324

101
113
321
323

101
113
321
323

Taipei

Wall hanging. Size 126 × 126 cm (49 × 49 in.) 1991
Privately owned
Design on page 99

Fire

Wall hanging. Size 108 × 72 cm (42 × 28 in.) 1989
Privately owned
Similar designs on page 107

324
343

113
324
344

113
324
344

324
344

324
344

324
343

324
344

114
324
344

114
344

114
324
344

114
344

114
324
344

114
324

114
324
344

114
324
344

Spring in Culham

Wall hanging. Size 172 × 140 cm (68 × 55 in.) 1989
Privately owned

Culham is a small village south of Oxford, near the River Thames.
Like so many English villages, it is full of daffodils in spring.

Photo by Raymond Faber, Luxembourg

7

Catherine's Wheel: Parallelograms

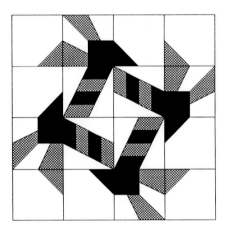

During my study, inspiration for new tiles has come from many sources, everything from carpets to chimneys. Tile number 256 was inspired by a photograph my son took of the dome in York Minster in the north of England. It is like tile number 341 in chapter 2: too busy on its own, so supporting tiles are needed. As so often before, a simple tile like 211 is the perfect partner, giving some very striking blocks. It should however be said that these blocks (pages 110 and 111) aren't particularly well suited to being repeated, so try and make other use of them. My first thought was to use the blocks for cushions, but I have a long history of starting with a small project like a pair of potholders and ending up with a quilt, so having made the first three cushions, I started

looking for ways of joining them. The end result can be seen on page 113, which can best be described as a sort of sampler quilt showing five different blocks.

Mixing 256 with 245 (see page 115) creates an effect like circles. The idea of making curved designs without employing curves can be a passion in its own right, and we will return to this phenomenon in chapter 9.

Number 251 is another one of those tiles that creates numerous designs on its own. Pages 116 and 117 concentrate on rotating blocks, whereas page 118 shows examples of simple repetitions of the basic set of tiles. Number 251 is also one of the few tiles that produce equally attractive results whether you apply plenty of colours or only a few.

Tile 211   *Tile 245*   *Tile 251*   *Tile 256*

211
256

211
256

211
256

211
256

211
256

211
256

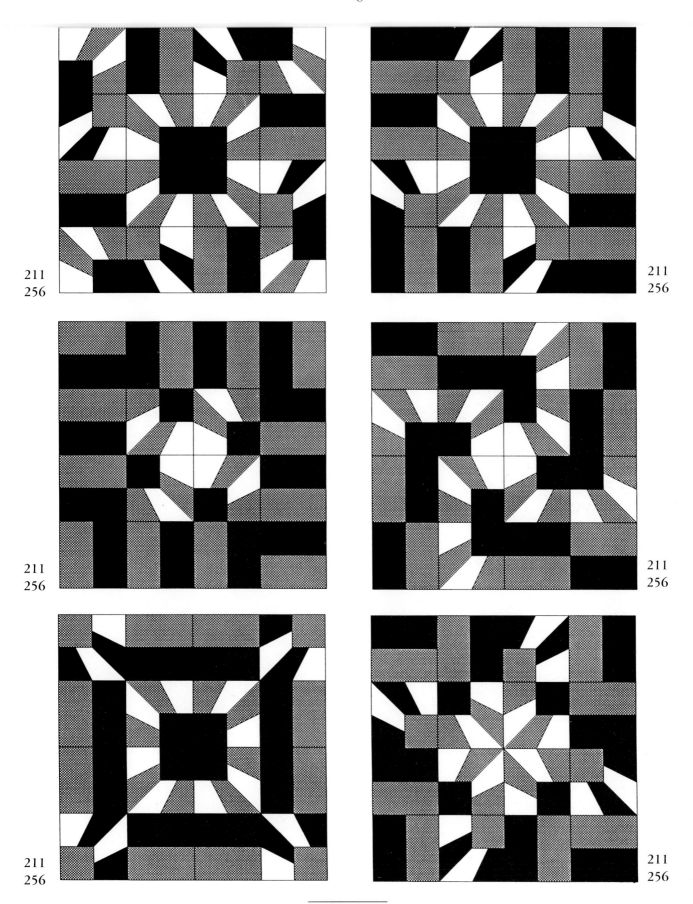

211
256

211
256

211
256

211
256

211
256

211
256

211
256

211
256

Catherine's Wheel

Wall hanging. Size 155 × 140 cm (61 × 55 in.) 1991

212
256

212
256

245
256

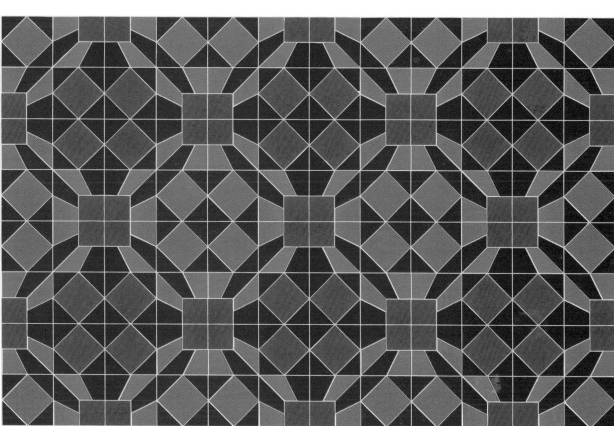

245
256

251

251

251

251

212
251

212
251

212
251

212
251

251

251

251

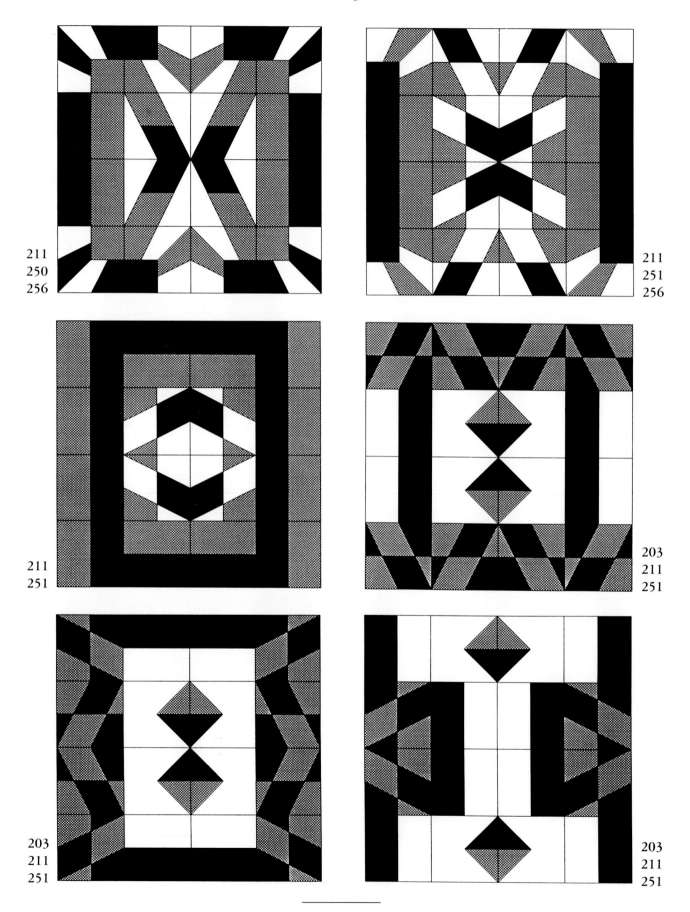

211
250
256

211
251
256

211
251

203
211
251

203
211
251

203
211
251

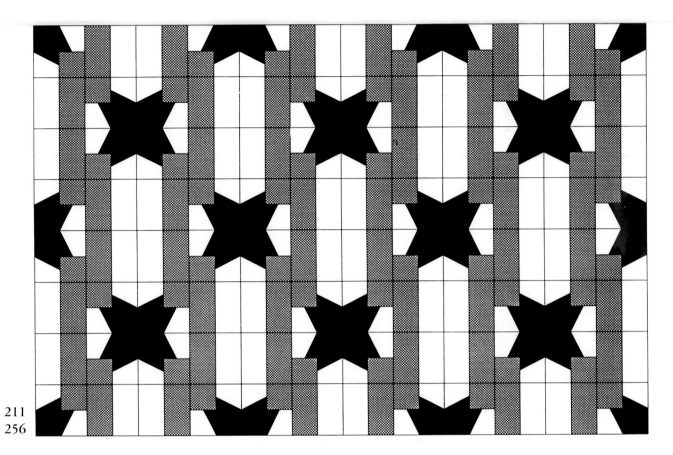

211
256

211
256

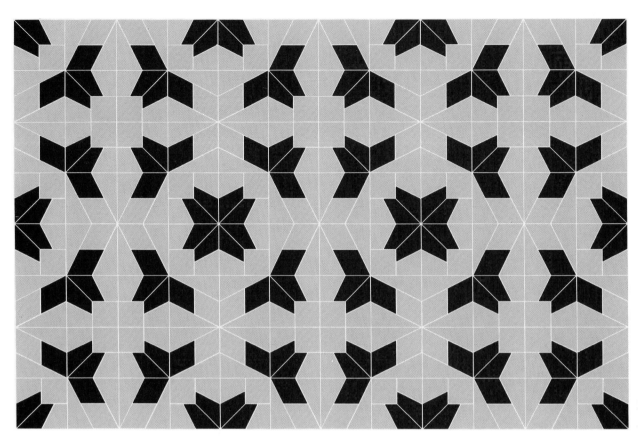

250
256

250
256

8

The Road to China: Stripes

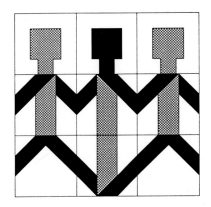

ooking at the various tiles in the Tile Library at the end of the book, particularly those based upon 3 by 3 or 4 by 4 grids, you may notice that many of them can be seen simply as stripes going across the square, sometimes straight across and sometimes turning a corner or two on the way. Extensive study of these tiles has revealed several types of designs based solely upon stripes. One such family will be the topic of chapter 10, but right now we will focus on tiles 347, 348 and 350. They are closely related, and they often give an effect as if several layers of stripes are placed on top of each other, similar to the designs in chapter 6. A supporting tile is 324, its main effect that of extending features already present in a design.

On pages 126 and 127 you will find four random-type designs. Striped random designs will often con-

tain interesting details that can be exploited on their own, but they can also form the basis of unusual works like Tove Bonnichsen's wall hanging shown on page 129. Tove has made several changes to the original design, removing some stripes and adding others. Similarly, if you find some of the designs in this chapter too complex or overwhelming, try removing a stripe or two.

This chapter also contains a couple of kaleidoscope designs. Striking as they are, they also demonstrate how you have to contend with particularly complicated tiles along the diagonals.

The four blocks on pages 136 and 137 are very complex. I suggest you spend a few moments convincing yourself that they are indeed all made from one single tile, number 348. My experience is that these designs are best used on their own.

Tile 324   *Tile 347*   *Tile 348*   *Tile 350*

123

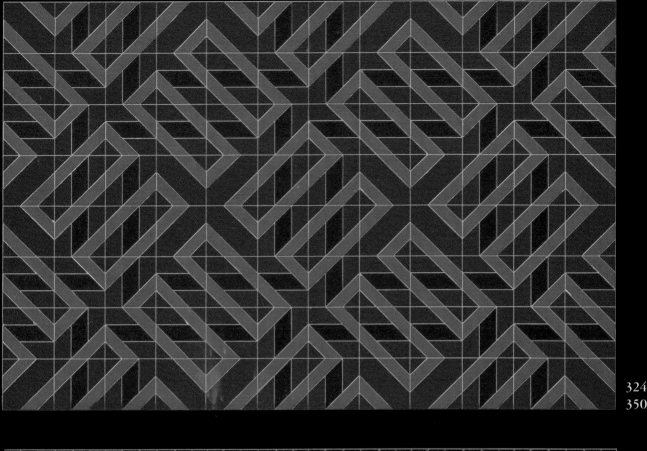

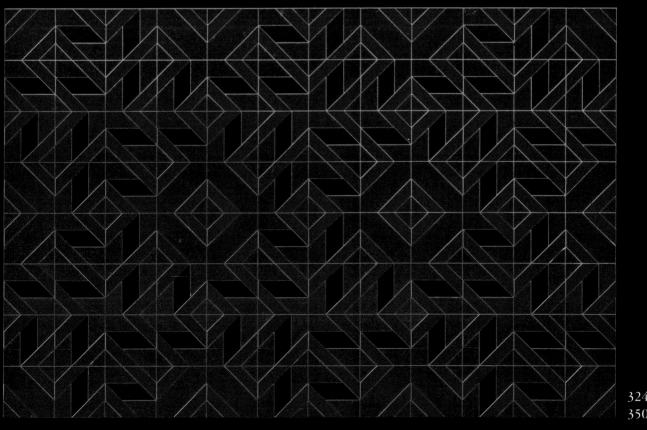

347
348

324
347
348

350

350

350

350

350

350

The Road to China

Wall hanging by Tove Bonnichsen
Size 165 × 118 cm (65 × 46 in.) 1990
Machine pieced

350
351

350
351

324
350

324
350

324
350

324
350

324
350

324
350

348
350

Where most designs are shown as 3 by 2 blocks, this one has been
extended to 3½ by 2½ blocks by adding one tile all the way around.
This is done to get more copies of the main feature of the design – the
twisted band made from three small squares.

324
348

324
348
350

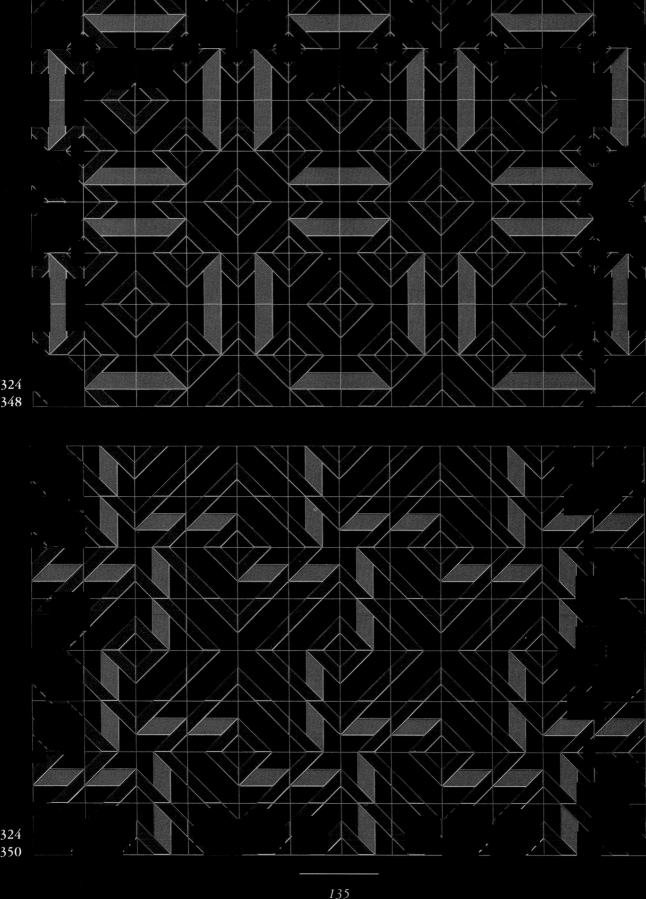

324
348

324
350

348

348

348

348

350
376

9

Sea Ways: Circle Lines

C hapter 7 showed a couple of examples of circles made without the use of curved tiles, and without having to piece any curved seams. I have always found this kind of design attractive, and they are quite easy to achieve. Tile number 248 – the Storm-at-Sea tile – is a good example of a circle-making tile. When used alone, it produces a sort of octagon, but the effect can be further exploited through the addition of triangles, squares or more complex tiles.

Several examples can be found on pages 140, 141 and 146.

For more elaborate curved designs, the V-shaped tiles number 376 and 452 have proven superior. Not only do they make overlapping circles and circles with intricate designs inside them, they are also the basic ingredients in the more complicated curves that are created when the basic set of tiles is rotated rather than mirrored. Several examples can be found towards the end of the chapter.

Tile 248   *Tile 376*   *Tile 452*

248
291
292

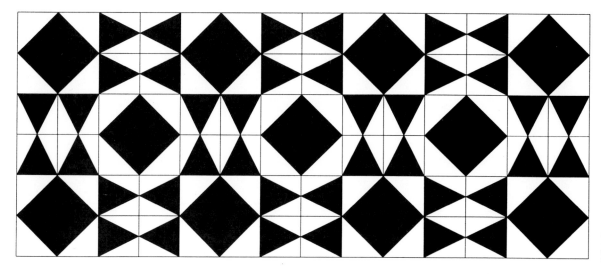

102
248

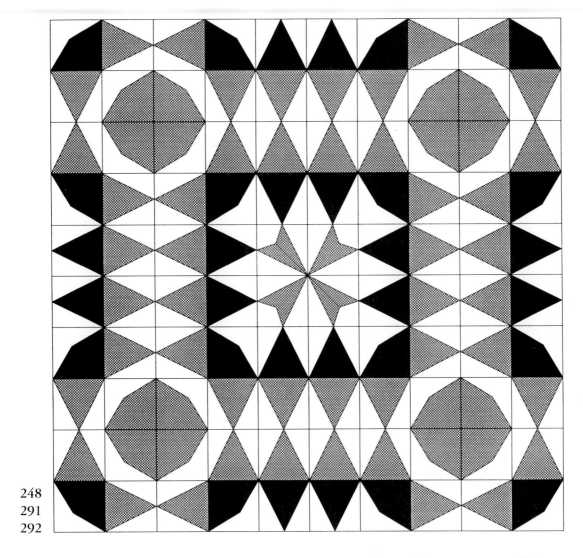

248
291
292

248
291

102
395

102
248
395

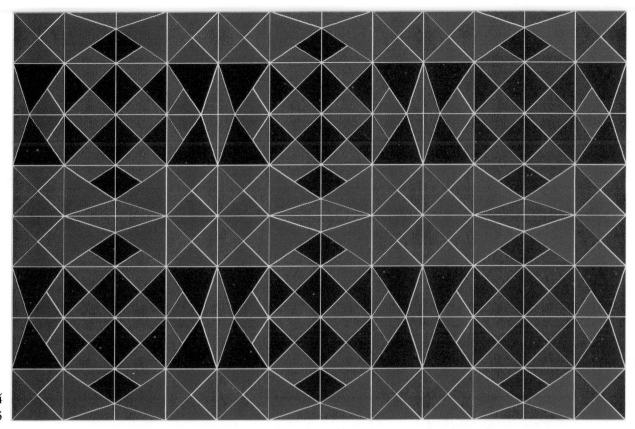

114
395

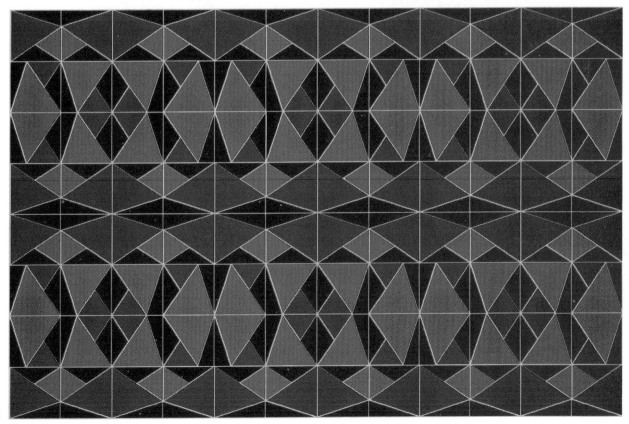

395

376
384

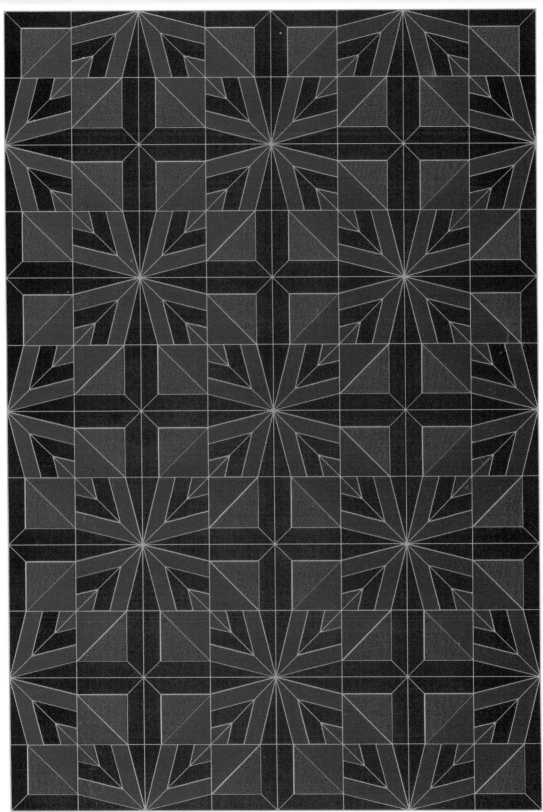

452
463

Seaways

Single quilt by Tove Bonnichsen
Size 195 × 147 cm (77 × 58 in.) 1990
Machine pieced
Design on page 140

376
384

328
376

328
376

328
376

452
463

328
376

328
376

328
376

328
376

328
376

328
376

328
376

328
376

328
376

328
376

10

Pain(t)staking: More Stripes

This chapter on stripes differs from other chapters in that no supporting tiles are involved. All tiles used are equally important, creating very strong designs. Many of them are well suited for piecing in just two colours.

The design at the bottom of page 156 was used for Pain(t)staking. It reminded me of paint brushes, so it is intended to show a lot of different-coloured paint brushes all painting black and white!

Even looking at a couple of blocks placed next to each other on a page, it is very difficult to imagine what would happen if we made a new design by alternating the two, mixing the blocks like on a chess board. Try looking at the two blocks on top of page 160 and then turn to page 166 for the answer! The design on page 167 is also made from two different blocks, this time taken from the centres of the two kaleidoscope designs at the bottom of pages 168 and 169.

The designs on pages 170–173 can be seen as flowers and leaves, making bold but at the same time delicate designs.

Note that the size of the basic set of tiles in the design on page 173 is 2 by 3, rather than the usual 2 by 2 or 2 by 4.

The two designs at the bottom of page 172 were used for the tablecloths shown on page 6 and page 174.

430
450

431
450

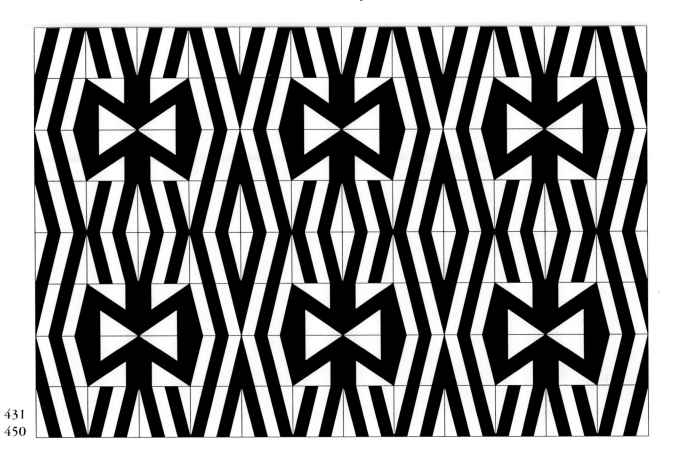

431
450

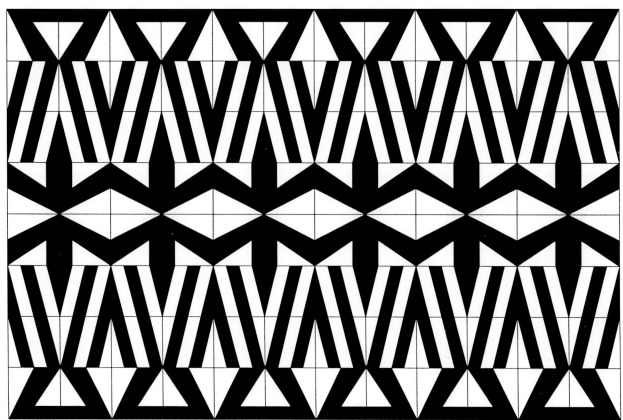

430
450

436
450

436
450

436
450

436
451

436
450

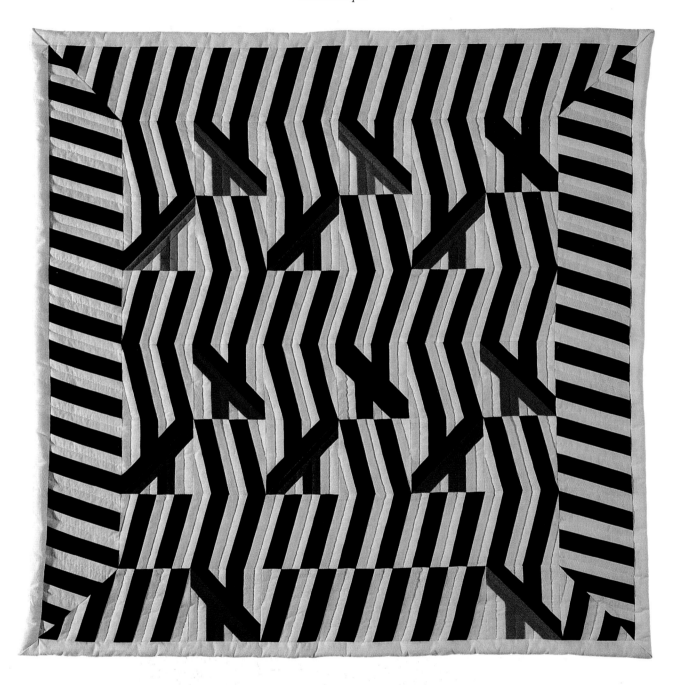

Pain(t)staking

Wall hanging. Size 100 × 100 cm (39 × 39 in.) 1991
Design on page 156

AA

Wall hanging by Tove Bonnichsen
Size 152 × 78 cm (60 × 30 in.) 1991
Design on page 156

417
450
452

417
450
452

450
454

454

454

417
450
452
454

454

454

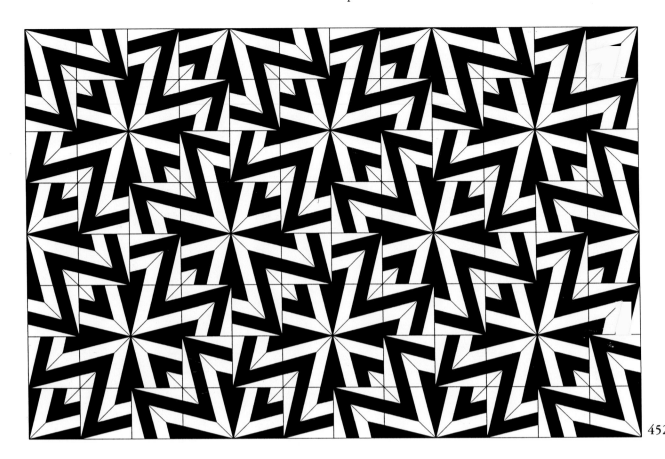

452

452
453

452

452
453

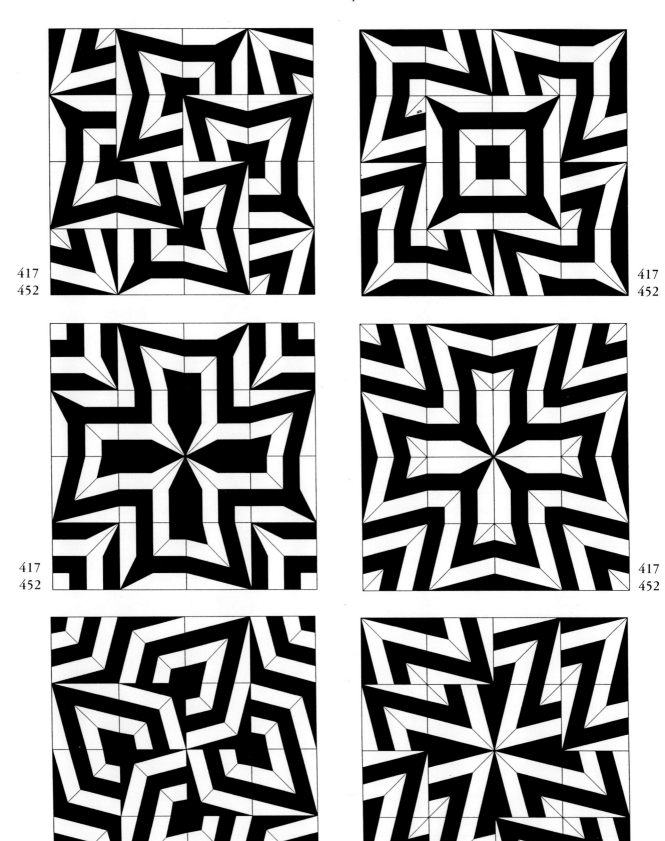

417
452

417
452

417
452

417
452

452
453

452

417
452

417
450
452

450
453
455

450
452

450
452
455

450
455

450
453
455

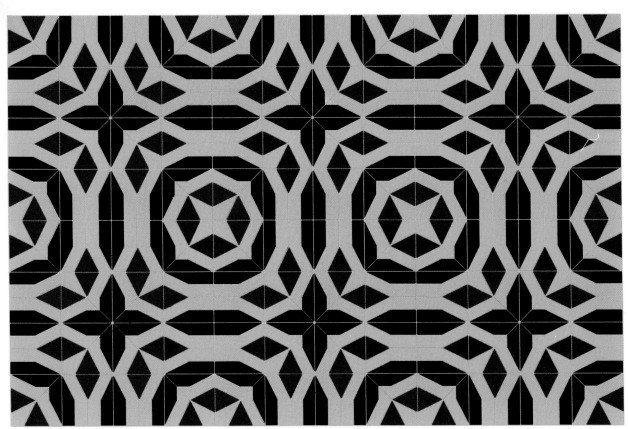

421
423

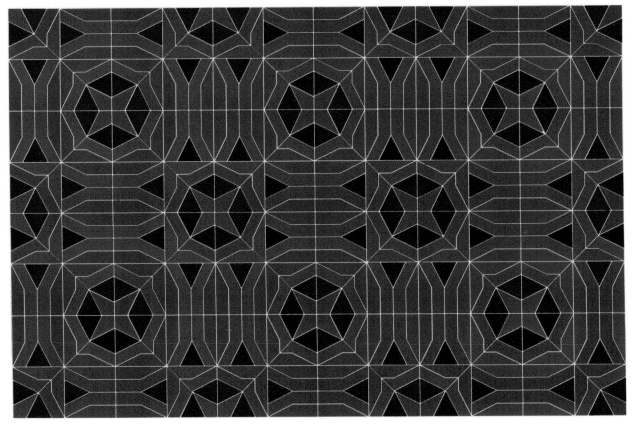

421
423

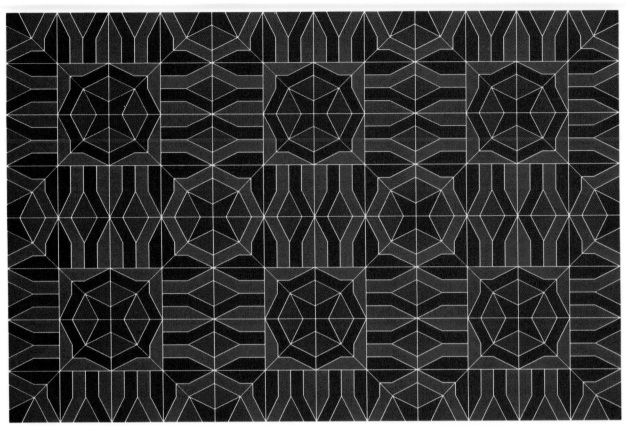

421
423

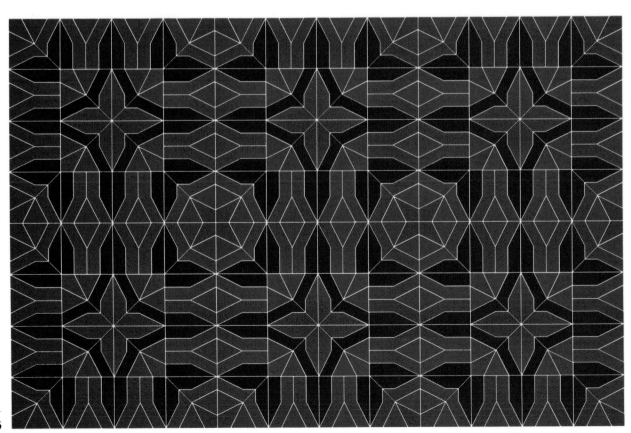

421
423

416
421
423

416
423

421
423

421
423

417
421
423

417
421
423

401
416
423

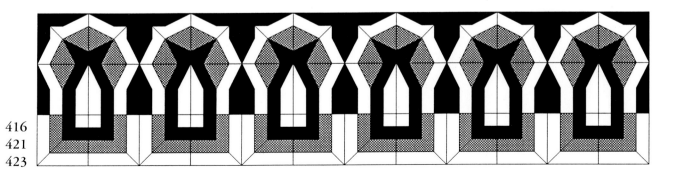

416
421
423

Summer 1991

Tablecloth. Size 132 × 132 cm (52 × 52 in.) 1991
The colours are inspired by wild flowers blooming in Denmark during
the month of July.
One-quarter of the design is on page 172, lower left

11

Winter Butterflies: Points

The theme of this chapter is the four-pointed star that emerges when four copies of tile number 466 are joined, and variations thereof.

Tile 466 is my Butterfly tile! It has been used on its own to create Flying Summer (pages 187 and 188), a very light design. A minor variation of 466 is tile number 389, which I've used in Winter Butterflies. This tile is more complex and requires a lot of piecing. To be quite honest, if I had to make Winter Butterflies again, I would make the basic templates bigger. I forgot the basic rule that the more pieces you have, the heavier a quilt!

Look at pages 176 and 177 and see what happened when the Attic Window tile was swapped with my Butterfly tile: the designs become much more delicate.

Pages 184 and 185 show further examples of mixing blocks.

Tile 389

Tile 463

Tile 466

453
463

452
463

453
466

452
466

453
463

417
452
453
466

390
466

389
466

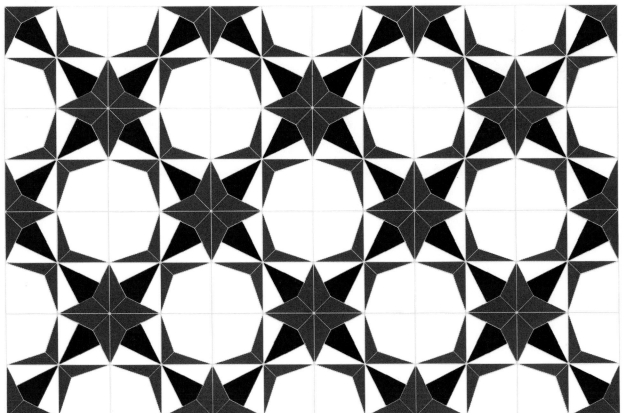

389
466

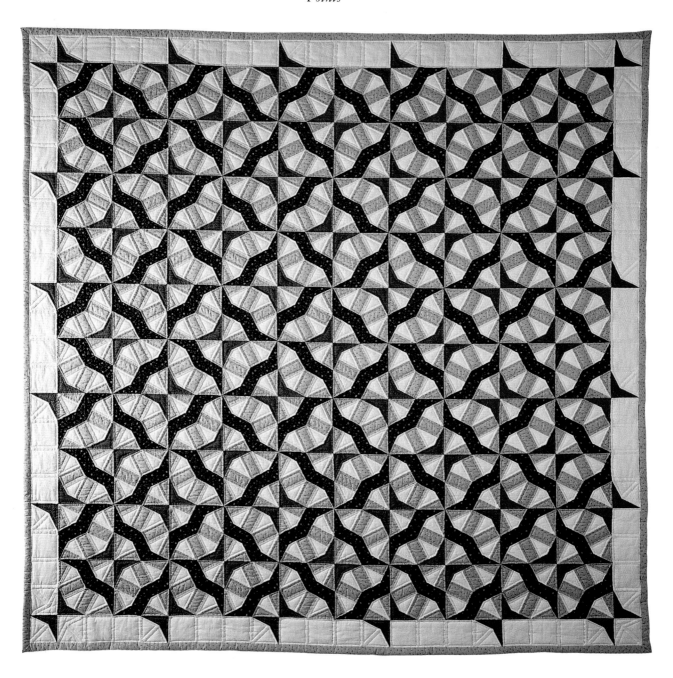

Winter Butterflies

Blue butterflies flying over cracked ice
Double quilt. Size 225 × 225 cm (88 × 88 in.) 1989.
Design on opposite page, upper right

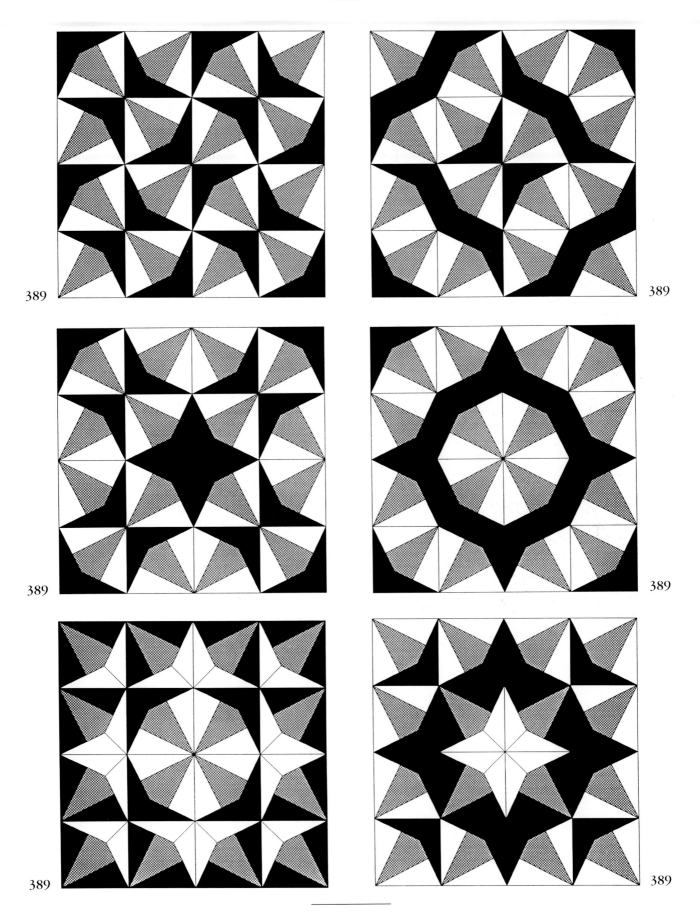

389

389

389

389

389

389

389

388
389
390
466

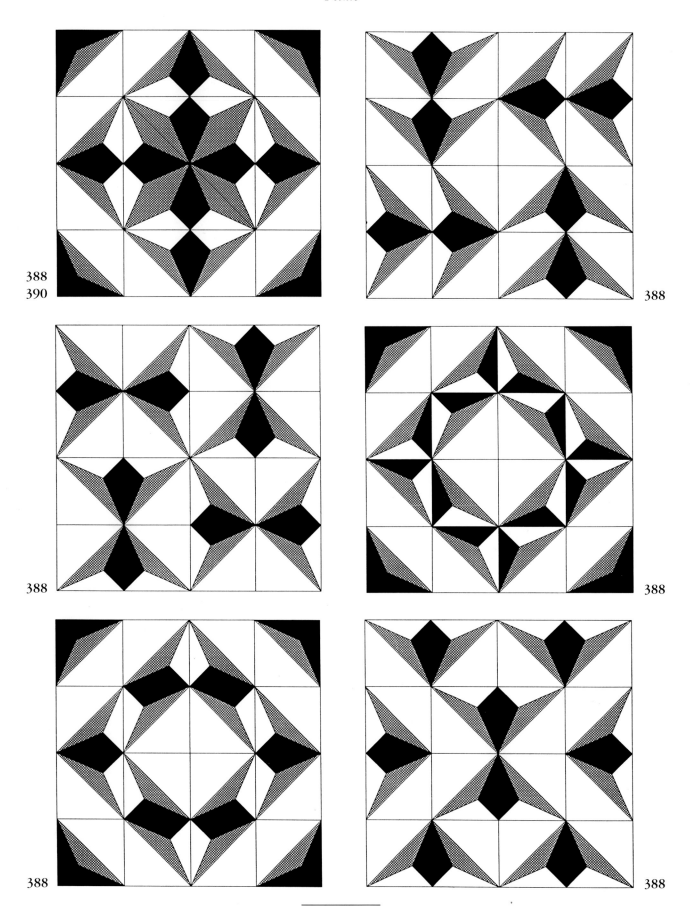

388
390

388

388

388

388

388

466

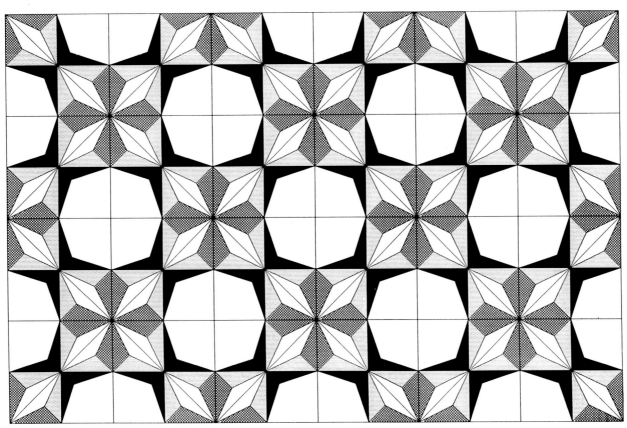

390
466

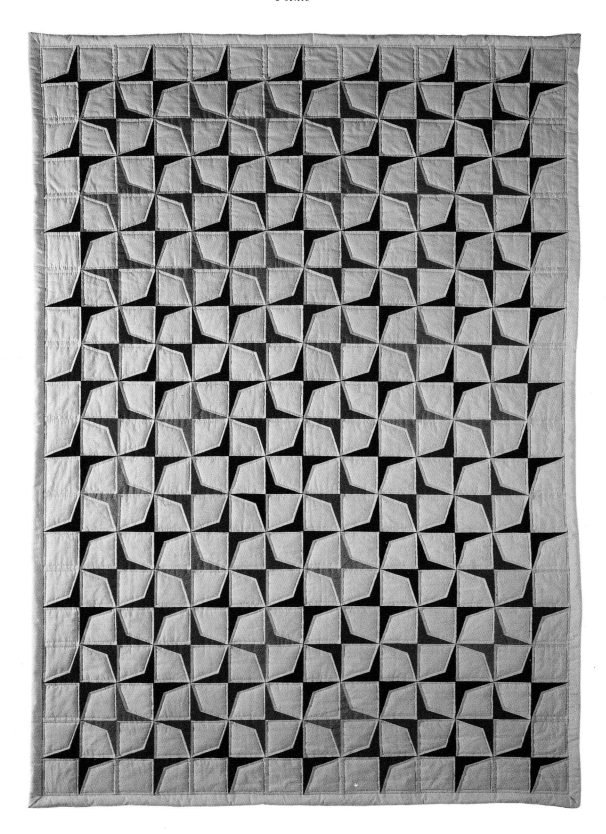

Flying Summer

Single quilt. Size 200 × 140 cm (78 × 55 in.) 1991
Design on page 187, top

Tile Library

You will see that the numbers on the tiles shown here are not consecutive. I have developed and computerised approximately 500 tiles, only a selection of which can be used effectively in one book. As you work, just keep in mind that the numbers shown with each design in the book correspond to a tile shown here in the Tile Library.

The Most Basic Tiles

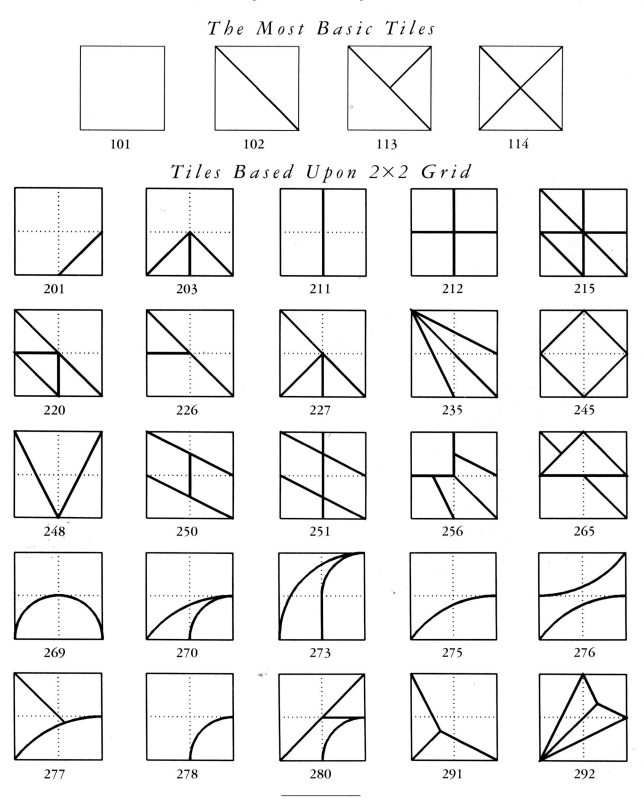

101   102   113   114

Tiles Based Upon 2×2 Grid

201   203   211   212   215

220   226   227   235   245

248   250   251   256   265

269   270   273   275   276

277   278   280   291   292

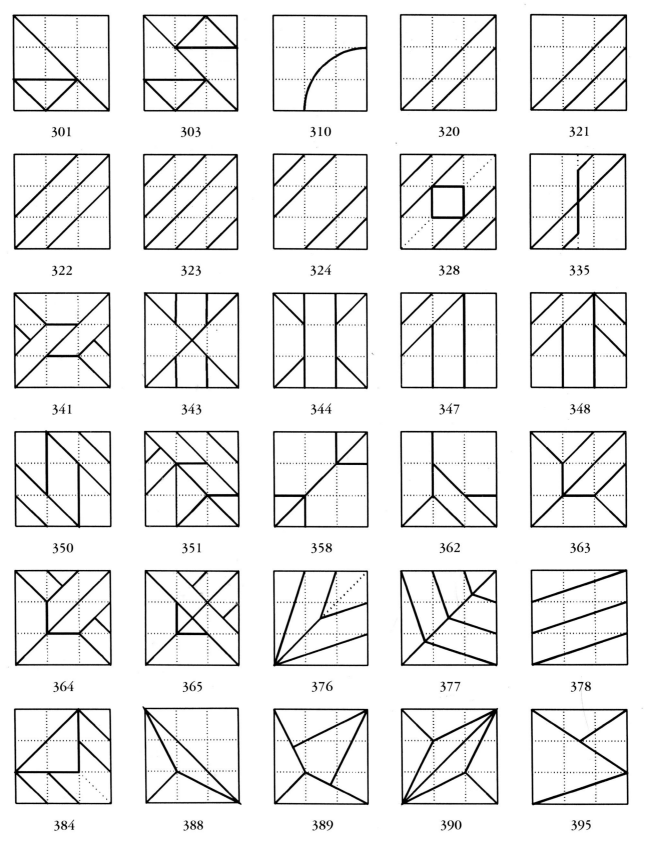

301 303 310 320 321

322 323 324 328 335

341 343 344 347 348

350 351 358 362 363

364 365 376 377 378

384 388 389 390 395

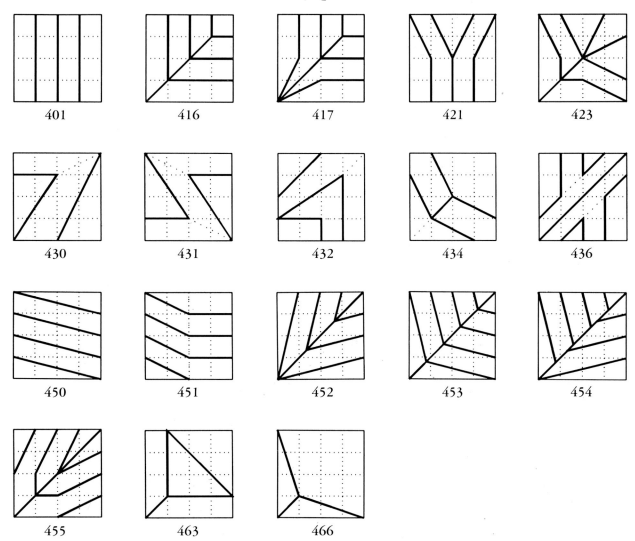

401 416 417 421 423

430 431 432 434 436

450 451 452 453 454

455 463 466

Acknowledgements

I would like to thank Thea de Kock and Ole Seyffart Srensen for all their support; Tove Bonnichsen, a fine patchworker who through keen interest, honest criticism and her realisation of so many fine designs has been a source of constant encouragement; my daughter Charlotte for helping me with the English language; Paul Biddle for his excellent photography; and Vivienne Wells, who guided me gently while giving me the freedom to create the book I wanted.

I would also like to thank those people who allowed me to borrow their quilts for illustrations.

Index

Page numbers given in *italic* refer to illustrations.